I WILL NOT BE BROKEN

I WILL
NOT
BE
BROKEN

FIVE STEPS
TO OVERCOMING
A LIFE CRISIS

◆

JERRY WHITE

ST. MARTIN'S PRESS New York

www.stmartins.com

Design by Patrice Sheridan

ISBN-13: 978-0-312-36895-1
ISBN-10: 0-312-36895-X

First Edition: May 2008

10 9 8 7 6 5 4 3 2 1

I dedicate this book to

Kelly Gammon White.

◆

CONTENTS

◆

	Introduction	1
1.	Everyone Has a Date with Disaster	9
2.	My Date with Disaster	20
3.	Step 1: Face Facts	34
4.	Step 2: Choose Life	57
5.	Step 3: Reach Out	77
6.	Step 4: Get Moving	96
7.	Step 5. Give Back	116
8.	Escaping the Victim Trap	139
9.	Building Resilience to Tragedy	151
10.	Helping Others Get Through Catastrophe: Or, How to Not Make Things Worse	161
11.	Survive. Inspire. Thrive!	184
	Acknowledgments	203
	Notes	207

I WILL NOT BE BROKEN

INTRODUCTION

♦

My name is Jerry White, and I'm a cofounder of Survivor Corps. It's an organization that helps victims of war and terror. Our mission, and my passion, is to help survivors heal and get on with their lives. Sounds simple, but in many places where we work, the idea of overcoming doesn't always resonate.

I came to this work as a result of big and small things that happened to me over the course of my life. One of the biggest happened on April 12, 1984. I was twenty years old, and I stepped on a landmine during a camping trip in Israel. Physically, it took a part of my leg. But it also divided my life in two—everything became either *before* or *after* the accident. It also taught me important things about resilience and coping that would later be the impetus for my work with survivors. I learned to walk on a fake leg, and then how to live and be happy despite the horror of that minefield. I returned to school, got married, had children, and worked hard to support my family.

Then, in 1996, I took a trip to Cambodia. As I moved around the country, I saw amputees literally on every other corner. This was a country that had been decimated by decades of conflict, leaving behind millions of mines and other explosive military litter. It sounds shallow, perhaps, but I realized then that I was not the only one with a date when life had exploded. As I walked along the streets of Phnom Penh, a little girl hopped up to me. She couldn't have been more than eight or nine years old, clearly not a former combatant in the wars of Cambodia. She smiled broadly at me, pointed at my $17,000 prosthetic leg, and said, "You are one of us." She leaned on her homemade crutch, and I realized she was right. I asked myself what I could do to help support that little girl and the hundreds of thousands like her—people who, through no fault of their own, had slammed into some kind of horrible date with destiny. I had strength; maybe I could give some of it to others and help them on their journey to recovery. So I began to build a support network for survivors. My thought was: We have all been through various struggles, so let's lend our support and strength to each other.

We called this effort the Landmine Survivors Network. Corralling the voices of mine "victims" around the world, we set out to ban the use of landmines and help survivors get legs and find work. This mission has sent me around the world, to the floor of the United Nations, the halls of Congress, foreign embassies, palaces, and local hospitals. Along the way, I've met a great many survivors from all walks of life. We've had very practical conversations about what works and doesn't work as we seek to achieve success in our lives . . . to walk a path of growth and renewal.

With this book, I share what I've learned.

They say what doesn't kill you makes you stronger. It's not

quite that simple. I believe you have to *decide* it will make you stronger. Experience has taught me that happy endings can never be taken for granted. They must be chosen. When I was in the hospital for six months in Israel, no one did my physical therapy for me. No one underwent the pain or the fear of six operations for me. I would have liked for someone to, maybe. I confess, the first time I was put in a wheelchair, I sat there and waited for someone to push it for me. I had just had another surgery, I was weak, in pain, exhausted. And when I looked up at my nurse, she looked down at me and laughed. "If you want to move, push." And so I did. And I continue to do.

Whether we like it or not, personal determination is required to build resilience—to become fit for whatever the future may hold. We have to tap inner resources and develop some emotional muscle. It's both a discipline and our responsibility. No one can do it for us.

The good news is, we are not alone. We are surrounded by survivors who have gone before us, and their examples will help mark the way forward. Their experiences show us that with the right support, *everyone* can recover and thrive. As we overcome hardship, there is laughter and hope and love waiting for each of us. But it is crucial for us to *want* those things. Frankly, I have always craved those things. And life has treated me pretty well.

It started with one of the all-time greatest childhoods. Born the fifth of sixth children, I grew up in a small picturesque coastal town about twenty miles south of Boston. Imagine an ocean, rocky coastline, and lots of neighborhood friends who played tennis in the spring, raced sailboats and practiced diving in summer, and played hockey on frozen backyard ponds in the winter. Ours was an Irish-American immigrant story.

My great-grandmother bought a milk cow, which led to another, and another, and voilá: a milk business—*White Brothers, Inc.*—was born, and within twenty years became the largest dairy in New England. I am now fifth-generation American, one of nearly three dozen cousins. We all went to decent schools and had summer jobs. I was lucky and I knew it.

But even into this idyllic small-town life, pain and sadness intruded. I grew up seeing plenty of evidence that bad things happen to good people. My friend's father shot himself. Two high school classmates died in a car crash. Another was paralyzed in an accident. Two friends almost died of starvation; another cut his wrists; one hung himself. My siblings and I went to a lot of Irish wakes and funerals. It was all part of the fabric of life, but I wondered: Why so much tragedy? Inside our home, my immediate family wrestled with the effects of alcoholism and a broken marriage. Both my grandfathers died before I was born. I remember watching my grandmothers fade to early deaths, one from Parkinson's, the other from drinking and heart failure. There always seemed to be some relative or neighbor fighting diabetes or cancer. How strange, I thought, that no matter how great life was, it was peppered with death and loss.

Even as a kid, I asked, "Why?" Why do bad, sad things have to happen? Silence answered. So, I thought, I guess life is unfair; bad stuff just happens. This was a very unsatisfying conclusion. I simply couldn't answer the toughest of life's questions—the *why* of it all.

So I began to ask a different question: *How?* Given that bad things happen, *how* did people absorb the blows and move through them? It's a question I have been asking for a long time, and I think I've discovered some answers. They've emerged from knowing and working with remarkable human beings around the world, hundreds of survivors and friends who have muscled their way through tough times and emerged stronger, wiser, and even grateful for their struggle.

We all admire individuals who do more than just "get through" tough times. We are awed by those who somehow emerge stronger from crisis, with their dignity and grace intact. These people somehow seem *more* at peace in their crisis aftermath. Can that be you or me? Can we put ourselves onto that list of people who have come through suffering and found a way to really live again? The question becomes: How do we not only survive but *thrive?*

Is there really a way to grow *stronger* in crisis? You bet there is. I am convinced we not only can toughen under pressure, but also soar. Why? Because I did. And I have watched thousands of others transform tragedy into growth. Over the past twelve years, I have made a global study of survivors. I've seen evidence that, regardless of misfortune and injury, individuals come out the other side full of life, love, and ambition to *do* something with their lives. I am inspired to know people all around the world picking up the pieces, rebuilding their lives, and learning to thrive.

So, how do they do it?

In the pages that follow, you'll learn. You will read, in their own words, just how they manage to thrive in the face of catastrophe. And as you'll see, it *is* something they choose to do, just as you can choose to do it. Success has more to do with how you think than with how you feel.

As my wife reminds me, "We can't change what's happened, but we can change our minds about it." The main challenge is always inside us. We can't change the facts—I'm sick, I'm betrayed, whatever—but we can change what we think about these facts. But only if we want to. Unfortunately, too many people are embracing victimhood these days, because it's easier to sit back and be inert. Life is just too short and beautiful for us to stay victims . . . to stay catatonic.

Because life will happen to all of us. Violence and terror can be visited upon just about anybody these days. Life explodes, and nothing is ever quite the same. I'm not just referring to a personal injury or illness, but also to the world, where headlines of terrorism, violence, and natural disaster assault us with increasing frequency. Some of us seek consolation in the belief that tragedy is happening *somewhere else*, far away. But, eventually, the bell tolls for you.

I have spent my entire working life focused on issues of Middle East peace, arms control, security, and humanitarian aid. As I've crisscrossed the world, visiting community after community ravaged by war, I've come to see that conflict has a face. It's not about the statistics of suffering, it's about the individuals who have been blown up, raped, and tortured. I've also come to see that "collateral damage" has a body—a body in constant pain that survives with scars, disfigurement, and missing limbs. I have worked with thousands of individuals who suffer the dual injustice of not only being gravely injured in the first place, but all too often becoming outcasts in their own families and communities.

All the while, I have been searching for that magic pill— some miracle cure that would help wounded people pick up the pieces, move forward, and rediscover life's fullness.

So how can we respond, in a *positive* way, to life's shocks and suffering? What's our goal when suffering comes? Because it *will* come.

Our goal is *life!*

The survivors I work with share a determination to live and a commitment not just to survive, but to thrive. Survivor

Corps is working with people who have been the most affected by man's inhumanity to man. And we are seeing the communities most affected by war and civil strife learning a better way to be. I believe there is no one better equipped to change the world than those most impacted by what's wrong with it.

My hope is that this book will both encourage and motivate—an invitation to get up and out the door. Far too many people respond to catastrophe by withdrawing. I understand that. It's normal and self-protective. Like snails, we pull back into our shells. But withdrawing, staying in isolation, will kill you.

No one survives alone. We need each other.

I hope my story, and those of friends I've met around the world, will flicker light in the dark tunnel where too many people feel trapped in pain. Even better, the survivor stories in these pages can teach all of us about moving forward. All of us need to learn to manage life's explosive moments. Life may change in an instant, like mine did in Israel, but instead of dreading them, I want to encourage all of us to honor our toughest dates—the tragedies that bind us—in an effort to transform victimhood into survivorship. Everyone feels vulnerability in the face of cataclysmic loss. But I will share what my survivor friends and I have learned, and maybe your own survivorship path will begin.

Over the past twenty years, I have met and talked survival with everyone from the famous—Diana, Princess of Wales, Elie Wiesel, King Hussein and Queen Noor of Jordan, John McCain, His Holiness the Dalai Lama, Lance Armstrong—to the not so famous but equally strong—Katie, Ken, Elizabeth, Colleen, and others. Each has something to teach us. They don't just get by. They thrive.

That's what I aspire to do.

Someday, if not today, you will need to understand this journey of survivorship, either for your own survival or that of a friend or family member. All of us will face trauma in our lifetime, whether it's the death of loved ones or another of life's unpredictable turns. It is a given that life will shock us.

This book offers the guidance you will need to recover and thrive after the worst happens.

1

EVERYONE HAS A DATE
WITH DISASTER

♦

We hate to call bad news normal, but it is. And no matter how hard you try, you cannot stay insulated from life's random acts. Chances are you'll get a phone call like I did several years ago. "Jerry, I don't know how to tell you this, but Dad is dead," my brother Ron said through tears. "He had a heart attack this morning." *Oomph!* It feels like a kick in the stomach. *Not this,* you think. *But he was just here for the holiday.* Nothing fully prepares you for these moments.

Disaster strikes in an instant, unwelcome and devastating. No one has yet figured out how to escape these sudden blows. Last year alone, there were more than 114 million visits to America's emergency rooms. Most of these hospital visits would count as sobering, if not traumatic, family moments. Each year, in the United States alone, roughly 6.5 million will become victims of a violent crime; 1.2 million will get professional help or die from drug or alcohol addiction; 1 million women will be raped; and over 31,000 will commit suicide.

No matter how you slice the numbers, they add up to a

hell of a lot of suffering and a lot of grief left in its wake. It reminds us just how normal it is to meet people in crisis *everywhere* in the world. We are all acquainted with grief. It is one of the things connecting us all, regardless of faith, culture, and geography.

But it's more than just pain that unites. The strength and resilience it takes to get through the pain also bind us. Scores of survivors of all types have shared their personal experiences with me for the purpose of this book: to offer a flashlight for dark times. These stories reveal different layers of survivorship, and drive home the point that *everyone* indeed has or will have a date with destiny, maybe even more than one. Knowing you have peers with similar experiences can be a great comfort. But why do some survivors handle their dates better than others? Why do some individuals grow *stronger* in the face of adversity, while others descend into bitterness and despair?

The survivor stories you are about to read are meant to help you face whatever adversity is in your life: the mother recovering from cancer, the family struggling with the death of a child, the father losing his spouse or a job, the sibling trying to make sense of an addiction or sudden accident that throws a family into turmoil. In these stories, you will see that in the wake of catastrophe, survival can sometimes be profoundly beautiful and inspiring.

Through my own experiences, including months of hospitalization and surgery after stepping on that landmine in 1984, I've learned what helped, and what didn't, as I found my own way forward. I've since worked with many survivors and trauma experts and heard thousands of stories of those who have overcome devastating loss, anger, and despair. My work since my trip to Cambodia has been a quest to find those things that help someone recover. I've seen that survivorship and resilience *can be learned*. With the right support, individuals can actually prepare themselves to cope with misfortune, resume life, and thrive.

This book illuminates the path to survival—five steps that can guide a person from tragedy toward a new life of renewed purpose and hope. The steps are not always sequential; they can be taken simultaneously. They can also spiral, skip, and repeat. Survivorship is different for each individual. But anyone who has overcome adversity and learned to thrive has come to understand the power of each step.

"No man is wise enough by himself," said Titus Maccius Plautus (third to second century BCE). That's why I've gathered wisdom from survivors living in all sorts of conditions and countries. I also draw lessons from historic figures, literature, and scripture—anything that sheds light on the path of survivorship. These lessons apply to anyone—the factory worker or farmer in small-town America, the wounded soldier abroad, or the high-powered lawyer in a city of millions. I believe these steps will guide you out of victimhood and on toward fulfillment:

1. **FACE FACTS.** One must first accept the harsh reality about suffering and loss, however brutal. "This terrible thing has happened. It can't be changed. I can't rewind the clock. My family still needs me. So now what?"

2. **CHOOSE LIFE.** That is, "I want to say yes to the future. I want my life to go on in a positive way." Seizing life, not surrendering to death or stagnation, requires letting go of resentments and looking forward, not back. It can be a daily decision.

3. **REACH OUT.** One must find peers, friends, and family to break the isolation and loneliness that come in the aftermath of crisis. Seek empathy, not pity, from people who have been through something similar. Let the people in your life *into* your life. "It's up to me to reach for someone's hand."

4. **GET MOVING.** Sitting back gets you nowhere. One must get out of bed and out of the house to generate momentum. We have to take responsibility for our actions. "How do I want to live the rest of my life? What steps can I take today?"

5. **GIVE BACK.** Thriving, not just surviving, requires the capacity to give again, through service and acts of kindness. "How can I be an asset to those around me, and not a drain? Will I ever feel grateful again?" Yes, and by sharing your experience and talents, you will inspire others to do the same.

Surviving the initial contact with disaster is only the beginning. What will we need to survive? No one thing can guarantee joy or fulfillment. But each step, sooner or later, will be needed to emerge from crisis alive and strong. With each step you will cross thresholds of pain, and then discover new possibilities.

Stories of disaster can be riveting. We find it difficult to turn away from the bloody details. But what comes *after* the trauma? The daily news may be filled with victims coming face to face with catastrophe. But how does life go on after the worst happens, the ambulance pulls away, and the sirens are muffled? Understandably, the marathon of recovery—months of pain and rehab—is much less riveting. Itemizing our symptoms can be boring or gross—"oversharing" tends to be a turn-off to our listeners. Unfortunately, full rehabilitation takes longer than most people's attention spans. That's why months after the funeral, the bereaved succumb to an overwhelming solitude. After a while, a siren might seem welcome, just for something to disrupt the melancholy.

I'm just describing what I observe—most of us have a hard time shoring ourselves up for the long haul of recovery. It is quite common for people to get stuck in their grief. But survival is our most basic human instinct. And if we are strong enough to stay alive after catastrophe strikes, then we owe it to ourselves and our loved ones to seek a way forward.

There is real suspense here. How will our stories end? Will we or our friends turn out okay? Life-and-death moments seize us, but personally I am more interested in the longer journey of life, rather than the emergencies. How on earth do we—do our loved ones—manage to find meaning again, to create order from chaos? How do we move on?

Each of us has a story. Though very few of us may face a war injury or battlefield, most of us have at some point had to deal with sudden life-changing loss, such as the death of a spouse or parent, hospitalization, physical disability, loss of love, or loss of work.

- Colleen and her sister are playing in front of their house when one of their best friends is run over by a truck, right in front of their eyes. Colleen learns to recognize how fleeting and precious life is, and wonders why her sister never recovers . . .
- Ken is on a mission in Africa to bring microcredit loans to villagers, and his jeep runs over a landmine. He wonders

whether the foot on the floor of the jeep belongs to
him or the driver. He calls for help . . .

- Karen learns her cancer has come back and spread, but
  she refuses to succumb to dark thoughts. She goes to a
  healer and tries something new . . .
- Irit picks up the phone in Israel and learns her son has
  been hit by a drunk driver half a world away and is
  brain-dead. Could she come and decide what to do
  with his body and whether to donate his organs? She
  boards the plane for New York . . .

It's not enough to survive these life-shattering moments;
we must live through them and move forward after them.
Everyone, if not now then eventually, has a date—the day
something blows up in our face, dividing life into before and
after. Things are never quite the same when the dust and debris settle.

It was Diana, Princess of Wales, who first made me ponder
the power of anniversaries and the deeper significance of our
dates. We were well into our second day of a trip together to
Bosnia-Herzegovina in August 1997. It was an exhausting
itinerary, driving in our white minivan through bombed-out
villages. I introduced Princess Diana to victims of all ages and
creeds—Croats, Muslims, Serbs, many of whom poured out
their gut-wrenching tales with tears and unfathomable grief.

One particularly emotional visit was to a home near Gra-
canica. The family was in enormous pain. The frail mother,
Mersiha, looked like she hadn't eaten in weeks. Her mother-in-
law could not stop wiping tears off her face. Mersiha's two
young sons were clinging to her as we approached. They were
only two and four. Two months earlier, their dad had gone
fishing. The war was over, and he had served heroically in the

Bosnian army, surviving the sieges and violence. It was such a relief to get back to normal. At last he could enjoy a quiet Saturday afternoon fishing on the banks of a river. He felt something catch on the line . . . a fish? He reeled it in. It wasn't a fish but debris from the bottom of the river. As he reached to pull it off his line, it exploded—the debris was an undetonated landmine, and it killed him instantly.

When we brought Diana into the home, the fishing tackle and rod were hanging on the living room wall. Mersiha's mother-in-law sobbed as she explained how her son had just appeared to her in a dream, consoling her, *Mama, it's going to be okay. You mustn't worry about me. Take care of yourself.* Mersiha then recounted the date in painful detail and distress. The emotion in the room was palpable, and Diana couldn't hold back her tears. There were no words, nothing to alleviate the pain of such a loss.

She climbed back into the back seat of our minivan and sat silently, looking with heavy eyes out the window. Ken Rutherford, my co-founder, and I were equally affected by the visit, and we joined Diana in silence. We resumed the journey, heading toward the next survivor destination. After some minutes, Diana sighed, then turned to me and said, "Everyone we meet, all the survivors tell me their date. They always mention their dates." Ken said, "Well, I'm December 16, 1993," the day his jeep ran over a landmine in Somalia. I added, "I'm April 12, 1984." There was a long silence. Then Diana said, "I'm July 29, 1981." She laughed, breaking the tension of all the pent-up emotions we had been feeling. She joked about her own date being the day she married. But what she had noticed was that there were definite "before" and "after" anniversaries. Days that came, and nothing was ever the same.

As we went from survivor to survivor, her astute observation proved true time and again. These dates weren't always tragic times, but times that fundamentally changed a person, a family, a community. And we found in talking to these people that it's all about what we do with a crisis *after* it occurs. Many feel trapped by what has happened to them, unable to move forward. We can get stuck on the events of one day. But today is a new day, and we have tomorrow to seize as well. Why not pledge, "This is the day I will become stronger"? Or, "On this date I will remember that my situation didn't destroy me, it made me a survivor"?

Princess Diana understood that to survive means to endure something that could have killed you or "taken you down." Like the loss of a son or daughter. Like stepping on a landmine. These are experiences terrible and terrifying. Such trauma presents a threshold. The outcome, positive or negative, is *not* preordained. We can do things to foster resilience and strength going forward.

Can you recall your date? Your own before-and-after moment, when life is cut in two by horrible pain or shocking news?

References to dates burned in our memory—when life is dramatically changed—appear in all kinds of survivor literature, including military battles, conquests, and political assassinations. Every American over fifty remembers where they were on November 22, 1963, when President John F. Kennedy was shot in Dallas.

One need only say "9/11" to transport us back to a day of tragedy and terror. Hijacked planes. Ground Zero. A hole in the Pentagon. A field in Pennsylvania. The final phone calls.

More recently, ask anyone who has lived in New Orleans what August 29 means, and they will recount the devastation wrought by Hurricane Katrina. It killed more than 1,600 people, destroyed 200,000 Gulf Coast homes, and displaced about 1 million people.

Most people, when telling stories of a crisis, will date their turning point. One 1990 survey found that 85 percent of people feel they have experienced such turning points.[1] It is not unusual for people to refer to other events in their lives relative to their more formative date. *That was the last time I saw her before the flood.* Or, *That was the year after mom died.*

Our dates are unforgettable because they change not only the facts of our lives—*I used to have a leg*—but our worldview and self-concept—*I come from a broken home.* They force us to redefine our expectations and attitude toward life. The emotions stay with us longer than the physical adjustments. In my case, I learned to walk again with an artificial leg in a matter of weeks, but didn't really get used to looking at my "residual limb" for years. It always surprised and slightly saddened me each time I caught a glimpse of it in the mirror after a shower or in the gym. *Is that stump really part of me? Where's the missing piece?* Likewise, some friends say it doesn't take long to learn to operate a wheelchair, but it does take time to learn to feel attractive, capable, and energetic again.

The anniversaries of these events can bring back powerful emotional memories. My mother, for example, calls me every year on April 12 to say, "I remember today, Jerry." It's one of her anniversaries, too.

The decisions we make after a crisis—the ways we choose to think about it—ultimately determine its impact on our lives. For some of us, the power of our crisis date doesn't conclude until its full impact is understood. The late Christopher Reeve recognized the same truth during his recovery from the horse-riding accident that rendered him paralyzed on May 27, 1995.

Juice (my nurse) thought my injury had meaning, had a purpose. I believed, and still do, that my injury was simply an accident. But maybe Juice and I are both right, because I have the opportunity now to make sense of this accident. I believe that it's what you do after a disaster that can give it meaning.[2]

For many people, there isn't one precise moment of crisis. There is no unexpected phone call to bring tragic news. It's what my friend Deirdre calls the "accumulation effect." A few unpleasant things overlap, and a crisis sneaks up from behind. Deirdre ponders her season of accumulated sadness in Montana:

> In my case, the world fell to pieces over a series of months with unhappy surprises. I learned that my husband's law practice was dissolving, and I had basal cell carcinoma on the end of my nose. Soon after, while half of the country protested the possibility, the U.S. government took us to war in Iraq. My eldest son was heading into high school and I could no longer pretend that I still had lots of time ahead with my children. By spring, what I had believed about who I was and where I sat in the world had been so nibbled away by these events that I found myself confused and in the midst of a depression that turned everything gray for another year.

Throughout history, people have struggled with low and high points. We all have a date or dates with destiny. But it's how we *respond* to our dates—life's anniversaries—that will determine whether we become true survivors who can fulfill our potential and ultimately thrive.

I am confident the example of my friends and fellow survivors will inspire you to persevere, to hold on for another minute, to try to imagine a future even after the worst has happened to you. You are about to meet survivors of all types, speaking in their own words. Their confessions of vulnerability may humble you, and their humanity will encourage you.

It may surprise you to find that you are one of us.

2

MY DATE WITH DISASTER

◆

April 12, 1984, was a sunny day in Israel. I was hiking the beautiful hills north of the Sea of Galilee. I'm not sure if I had ever been in a better mood. In fact, there was probably a smile on my face when I stepped on the landmine. I think I was humming at the time.

I was in college, and I had taken a year abroad to study in Jerusalem. I was determined to learn all I could about the history of religions in the Middle East. I had just turned twenty, and the only Hebrew words I knew when I boarded that flight to Tel Aviv in 1983 were *shalom* and *shekel*. At first I wondered how I would get through the year, but I loved it all—the Hebrew, the Arabic, the biblical archaeology. When the Passover break signaled that our time together was drawing to a close, we set out on one last improvised and rambling hike through northern Israel.

I go camping with two of my closest friends and Jerusalem roommates, David Kenyon and Fritz Balwit. David is a strapping pre-med Texan who says *"Shalom, y'all"* with a big smile, and Fritz is a maverick intellectual from Wisconsin who loves jazz and plays chess and classical guitar. We are all different, but get along great.

My friends and I are determined to see something off the trail of student tourism. After visiting the Banyas, a modest waterfall, we set off on our final hike, following an alluring path along the stream. We can see the hilly vista toward the east—the Golan Heights—and below us, toward the west, the flatter valley of northern Galilee.

Toward evening, we scan the horizon for a promising campsite. We spot a run-down fortlike shelter just off the trail at the crest of a sloping hilltop. Score! Upon investigation, it turns out to be abandoned Syrian bunkers, possibly relics from the Six-Day War. We are sitting atop the pre-1967 front line occupied and appropriated by Israel. We select the least ramshackle of the bunkers and set up camp, stretching out our sleeping bags on the dirt.

We start off the next morning bright and early. The tall grass and new spring growth are damp, but the day promises to be warm and clear. Fritz is the first to set off down the hill, cutting off from last night's path in a more direct line toward the road we see below us. He enters a sloping field, strewn with rocks. He notices it is marked on one side by the remains of a fence line but gives it no thought. I stride past Fritz quickly, making some snide remark about his stubby legs and slowpoke pace. David is pulling up behind us, probably giving voice to some song, as was his morning custom.

Even with my heavy pack, I feel light and full of happiness, to be together with my peers, heading for Jerusalem. I am probably only fifteen yards ahead of Fritz when the quiet morning is punctured by a loud thud. The earth opens and spits up at me, and I'm swallowed by dirt and rocks. The blast of soil in my face blinds me. I fall on my hands and knees. I am suddenly moving in a warp of slow motion. I picture my mouth open, coughing, screaming, but I don't hear anything. *What is happening? Is it a rocket? Are we being attacked by terrorists?* We're not that far from Lebanon, in fact, and I have read the accounts of Katusha rockets blowing up Israelis in the North.

Suddenly flushed by a blast of adrenaline, I begin yelling loudly. My voice emanates from my belly. *It sounds eerie, like a wounded animal.*

My breathing stops. I brace myself for another blast—the last moment of my life.

Silence.

Nothing happens. So I resume groaning to make sure that I'm in fact still alive. Between my cries for help I keep spitting. *I've got to get this shit out of my mouth. What's this metallic taste . . . so dry but still dripping red saliva?*

As the dust starts to settle, Fritz and David command me not to move. Something seizes me inside like cold steel. I freeze. My heart pounds inside my throat. Everything is blurry, with dirt stinging my eyes. Though motionless, I keep spitting blood and dirt.

David shouts to Fritz, "Jerry's stepped on a mine! Get up on a rock, Fritz, and don't move!" Fritz obeys and jumps on a rock, but just as quickly jumps off to meet David at my side, where they plead with me to be okay. No one wants to watch me bleed to death in this godforsaken field, on a perfect sunny day.

It dawns on me that we are in a minefield, whatever that is. *Didn't I read about these things in history books?* I have no idea what a mine looks like, or why there would be any here by our campsite. *Where are they? How can we spot them?* How to navigate a minefield is more on Fritz and David's minds than mine. They no longer move normally, but step gingerly, rock to rock.

They kneel at my side, breathing heavily. And as they roll me over, we see, for the first time, what landmines do. They maim. That's their job. "My" mine, I learned later, was laid in the ground by Syrian soldiers during the 1967 war, when I was only four years old. It waited dutifully for the moment it could shred my legs, tearing through my bones and muscle. And steal my right foot.

"Where's my foot? Where's my foot?" I am pleading. I keep chanting this over and over, as much panting for help and air as trying to get my own brain to comprehend this missing piece . . . there is nothing there. It does not seem to compute. No more toes. No heel or ankle in sight . . . just my blood leaking out of mangled, raw flesh.

"My leg!" The left one is torn apart, too. I see bone fragments sticking out of my calf, and I am curious to see the inside of my knee exposed. Surreal thoughts swirl in my head: *Wow, that shinbone looks so thin . . . Why do I have a sore throat? I'm soooo thirsty . . . Where is my passport? My blood tastes like the handlebars of my bike when I was a kid . . . The sky is so blue . . . This really hurts . . . God, where are you?*

Fritz is yelling for me, "Jerry, Jerry!" He has ripped off his shirt, but put on his jean jacket, for "protection" from another explosion (a move we joke about to this day). He is looking frantically for my missing foot, and only finds the remnants of my Timberland hiking boot. I see him pick it up with two fingers. How can the boot be mostly intact, with no foot remnants or flesh inside? All gone.

David, the pre-med student, rips off his white T-shirt and starts to wrap it around my lower right leg. It hurts a lot. The bone has sheared off, and a longish piece of heel flesh dangles from the bottom. The left leg is bleeding badly, with a piece of bone sticking into the calf, like a broken-off knife. Fritz holds my hand tight, repeating, "It's going to be okay." David pulls and tugs on the cotton T-shirt, soaked with my blood.

We really want the bleeding to stop. *Now*. We are starting to panic.

I hear a loud voice, like a shout in my clogged ear. *Quiet! You don't die this way. There is purpose.* The voice disappears as fast as it came. But it feels like a slap in the face, waking me up. Who said that? I somehow summon the faith to believe the voice. *All energy needed. No more groaning. It's time to focus.*

"How do we get out of here?" I choke out. "What do we do? We need help," I say unhelpfully. *No shit*. No one says anything. David and Fritz stand up and yell for "Help!" "Someone!" "*Tazor lanu!*" Help us! *Hello?* We keep at it, but there's no answer, no indication that anyone would hear. We are miles from the nearest town. So we pray, out loud, "Please God, help us."

Fritz and David struggle to move me, to pick me up. I'm six foot three and 195 pounds, so it's not easy. There's no sense retracing our steps. We are in the middle of a minefield and we don't know where it begins or ends. They decide to try to carry me out of the minefield by the most direct route—straight down the steepest, rockiest hill toward a dirt road to a kibbutz in the distance. The road is in view, anyway, and we might, by caution and incantation, Fritz thinks, luck out and escape stepping on another mine.

I am watching David and Fritz's faces, looking for clues of fear. Their eyes are darting, and they are sweating and straining each time they pick me up, wincing every time I wince. "It's okay, Jerry. Hang in there." We actually stop a moment to pray together, more urgently this time, for God's help. David re-members:

> Then we started down the hill. The grade was steep and rocky, and we stumbled and fell repeatedly. I was most afraid of you landing rear first on another landmine. I sensed that whatever else would happen from a detonation would happen to the three of us together. I vividly recall carrying you down that hill knowing that our fates were sealed as one if another landmine found us. As we stumbled our way down the hill, a military helicopter flew overhead at low altitude. We waved and shouted, but the flight path did not appear to change; we had no idea if they had seen us. As the grade of the hill flattened we encountered tall spring grass and briar patches, which were impossible to prevent from scratching your wounds.

With my arms clutching my friends' necks and shoulders, my shredded limbs are now fully in view as we push our way through spring brush. I cry out as my pant leg gets caught in briars, thorns tearing through my clothes and skin. Tears are now mingling with my sweat. Fritz places each foot down, step after step, with a whispered prayer and a shudder. *Dear Jesus.* I don't think David takes a deep breath for hours. Within a few steps, they stumble and I fall to the ground. They pick me up again. A few more steps. Another prayer, only to stumble again, this time dropping me on my bloodiest side. *Oh, dear God, I can't take this.*

Fritz and David maneuver me slowly to a nearby line of rock piles, hoping for safer ground. A short distance farther, we have our first view of a security fence, layers and coils of barbed wire directly in front of us.

Overwhelmed by the futility of stumbling over the stones toward a barrier we can't breach, David and Fritz sit on a pile of rocks trying to come up with a plan. I say someone has to go for help because I'm not sure I can take it—that is, being dropped again by my two friends. Searing waves overwhelm me. I beseech one of them to stay with me because I fear the brush is too high for someone to find me again, lying alone in a field. It's decided; David, the first-aid–savvy friend, will stay with me, while Fritz threads his way through the final fifty meters of minefield and out over the fence to run for help. Off Fritz goes, reeling, praying with each step, aware of the danger as his weight hits soft earth, wading through the tall grass. Finally, Fritz hauls himself over the top of the barbed barrier. David whispers, "He made it out," still alive.

It feels like several days have passed, but I later learn it's only been an hour or so.

I can't see a thing. I'm lying on my back begging David for a sip of water. I start twisting David's forearm with both my hands, squeezing tighter and tighter, in an obsessive manner, trying anything at all to distract me from my burning pain, and fear. *I want to hurt you, David, so I don't have to feel this all alone.*

On the other side of the fence, Fritz now sees the red metal signs, warning of *"Muqshim"*—mines! We're stupid American tourists hiking in a minefield. How the bloody hell did we get inside?

Half running, half staggering down the dusty road for no more than five minutes, a jeep comes into view, and Fritz hails it to stop. He explains what's happened. A weathered-looking Israeli nods. He had heard the blast and is prepared for the worst. They drive a minute or so back to the site. Without hesitation and with few words, the Israeli brings out his wire cutters and works his way through the fence. He and Fritz reenter the minefield. He admonishes Fritz to follow his previous steps, only vaguely apparent in the imprints among the grass nearer the road. The Israeli follows, putting his foot carefully down in each of Fritz's footsteps.

I hear voices, Fritz, and an unfamiliar Israeli accent. They yell to David, "Don't move!" I'm in agony but somehow calmer now. The Israeli has first-aid medical supplies with him. You already tied a tourniquet? David nods: "Yeah." Then these three lifesavers carry me out on a stretcher following the exact path Fritz made coming in.

Years later, Fritz writes to me, reflecting on the nature of this life-saving moment:

> A portion of my mind started to detach itself into a realm of pure observation. I watched the birds above me, and then as if from their vantage point, looked down on four men struggling on the wrong side of a security fence to extricate themselves from a stretch of earth polluted by the devices of war-making man. We got you through the fence and then waited for an ambulance that had been summoned by the Kibbutznik. I recall a huge sense of relief as we waited. You were remarkably calm at this point but descending into shock. A short time later, an ambulance arrived. Then the Israeli military police. The former took you away. You told me as we parted that you would be all right and not to worry. David accompanied you in the ambulance, while I was summoned by the police and Israeli Defense Forces to do a bit of explaining.

I was on a stretcher when the nurse's scissors cut off the remnants of my green army pants, and she asked me whether I was a soldier. *No, just dressing like one, I guess.* They rushed to prepare me for surgery. I begged for a sip of water, anything, even a corner of wet cloth to suck on, but the nurses knew I couldn't drink anything right before surgery to have a part of me sawed off. Some angel nurse took pity on me and slipped me a single Q-Tip dipped in lemon. *Hmmm, this is delicious.* I sucked the hell out of that Q-Tip. That one tiny thing made a world of difference somehow. It gave me an ounce of control.

David was still at my side:

A young Arab resident entered the emergency room. As he unwrapped the leg, he asked if I was bothered by seeing it. Of course I was, but by that point I was fairly familiar with the wound. When he saw the damaged leg, he sighed a lament. Then someone poured betadine over the open wounds, which obviously worsened the pain. A large gray-haired man, the surgeon, came in. He asked me to leave. I had reservations, but he made it clear I had to go. We bid farewell, and I went out to the waiting room which was empty. I sat down and took a breather. I didn't realize my jeans were soaked with your blood, and my shirt was also stained. I had no wallet and no money, just the clothes on my back. I remember a kind and beautiful lady came into the waiting room. As she sat, we talked a bit, and she offered me a glass of fruit juice. It was one of those small acts of kindness I still remember more than 20 years later.

I sat in the waiting room six hours with very little information. Finally, Fritz made it from the north wearing a shirt given him by one of the kibbutzniks. Fritz and I were directed to the hospital kitchen by the nurses since we had not eaten all day. I remember a few meager leftovers. As we sat there in the quiet, the events of the day caught up with me. I felt ill and searched for a restroom to no avail. I stepped out onto a sec-

ond floor balcony and barfed my guts out. I sheepishly re-
treated from the balcony when I noticed some Israelis look up
at me. I was standing just over the ambulance entrance.

I've always hated hospitals. Not that I had been in many.
Before getting blown up, I had never broken a bone or been in
an emergency room. I did have my tonsils removed at age
nine. My only memories of pain are absolutely minor.

One of the worst things about trauma is losing all control,
and dignity. You become a patient, not a person. The steering
wheel is yanked from your hands. And a catheter is forced into
your privates.

A couple of times each day a team of nurses and a doctor
would come by my hospital bed and unwrap the gauze around
my legs to inspect the amputation, and with sterile tweezers start
to pick out the shrapnel and tiny pebbles driven into my body by
the force of the blast. They'd pour alcohol and disinfectant over
my wounds. The doctors' visits terrified me, their white lab
coats, the inspections of my body. I'd beg for them to stop for a
minute so I could catch my breath, not pass out. I wanted to be
a man, but I cried like a baby. They handed me a plastic bedpan
every time I began dry-heaving. But nothing stopped them
from doing their job. I had lost control of my life.

It's hard to describe what it's like when someone draws
with a purple marker on your body where he will be sawing
through flesh and bone in the morning. *My* flesh. *My* bone. I
rage at the fact. No one has permission to steal a piece of my
body. *Okay, just sign the paper here and we'll wheel you over for the
X-rays before surgery.*

Trauma doesn't happen just to one person. Pain makes us
feel alone, but the shock waves reach across miles and oceans,

impacting family and friends. April 12, 1984, was a before-and-after moment not just for me, but for my parents, siblings, and friends. My mother still remembers it like it was yesterday. She is at home in Cohasset, 5,400 miles away, alone in a big house. She wrote in her journal:

> It is a beautiful day. The phone rings and I pick it up. Susan Jacobs, of the U.S. Embassy in Israel, is on the phone. My heart leaps into my throat. "There has been an accident. . . . Jerry is alive, but he has stepped on a landmine and his right foot was blown off." BLOWN OFF . . . BY WHAT? A LANDMINE? BUT ISRAEL IS NOT AT WAR . . . THERE AREN'T ANY LANDMINES THERE . . . Susan said Jerry was in a hospital in Safed, but he was out of surgery and OK . . . She had seen him. "OK"—what does she mean "OK"—I am in a huge panic. I did not believe this woman. . . . I thought she was trying to work into telling me Jerry was dead. But then she says she has set up a telephone connection, and for me to wait by the phone for the call . . . I had never felt so alone. The phone rang ten long minutes later. He really was there . . . I heard his voice . . . he sounded weak. I told him I was coming . . . he hesitated and then said, "It's OK, I was thinking you have been good in the past when I have been sick, you can come." I thought to myself . . . Jerry, you may be twenty years old, but you could not keep me away if I had to swim! I was relieved that he was alive but in shock at the severity of the accident . . . how did this happen?

> I quickly called my husband and the other five children. The shock, the tears, the hysterics were almost more than I could bear. They all made immediate plans to come to Cohasset for Easter. But I will not be there to comfort them; my flight left on Holy Thursday. I arrived in Tel Aviv at

3pm on Good Friday. For me that was appropriate, I was in my own agony, and I needed a Role Model.

The agony of that week, while I made arrangements to go to Israel, was only bearable because I was on the way . . . Nothing mattered except that I got there as quickly as I could. Did I really think I could make this better or take away Jerry's pain?

They say courage is fear holding on a minute longer. But it took a different kind of courage to look into the face of my grieving mother. Yet another thing I couldn't control. Every time I peered into her glassy eyes, my stomach tightened. Mom couldn't stop welling up and crying. She wanted to be in on every detail, to see and feel my wounds. "How do you feel today, my son?" she would ask each morning. *Mom, what type of question is that?* At one low point, in a moment I still regret, I kicked her out of my hospital room, swearing at her after she spilled my urine bottle on the floor and got all weepy again. "Stop it, Mom! The last time I checked, it was *my* leg that got blown off, not yours. Get out of here and go cry somewhere else!" She fled the hospital and didn't come back that night. Then I was the one crying. Where was she? She had gone for a long walk, for hours, feeling terribly alone and shaking her fist at me, at Israel, at God.

In the midst of your "explosion," you, like me, will be all over the map. There are days when you're stronger and calm, days when you're weak and rattled. But uppermost in my mind was the assertion that "I will be okay." It was my mantra of hope. I clung to the future.

Reflecting on my minefield experience with the distance of decades has helped me bring into focus what got me through. At age twenty, nothing had prepared me for this explosion of life. My upbringing had been peaceful, sheltered, if not idyllic. How could I know anything about surviving when I had hardly lived? They say the only way to get through something is to go through it. At first I just wondered if I would ever walk again. In retrospect, I can see how I needed to cycle through various stages of recovery, three steps forward, two steps back. Sometimes it felt like I was on a StairMaster, cycling and panting through all the steps, but feeling like I was going nowhere fast. I would skip over the steps at times, but I made steady progress as I climbed out of my victimhood, emerging stronger than before. I went through these steps of survivorship without knowing what they were.

1. **FACE FACTS.** My leg will not grow back . . . but I can still have sex. *Whew.*

2. **CHOOSE LIFE.** At twenty, I was definitely not done with life, laughter, and love.

3. **REACH OUT.** Friends and family taught me the power of staying connected.

4. **GET MOVING.** I graduated and made plans to move and find a job.

5. **GIVE BACK.** I had always tried in little ways, but was compelled eleven years after my accident to address the needs of war survivors much less fortunate than I.

Over the years, I thought a lot about what happened to me and how I got through. I also started to watch closely how other survivors get through, learning to thrive after the worst happens. Each of us has seeds of victimhood, survivorship, and thriving potential within us. The challenge we face is integrating our experiences—sorrowful and joyful—to help us evolve from victimhood to thriving.

We may all aspire to thrive, just as we would like to get in shape—fit for life. But are we willing to do the survivor exercises required to grow strong, using our past pain to foster our future growth? The next five chapters describe a path out of victimhood and onward toward thriving.

But before you continue, pause for a moment to admit to some vulnerability. Consider your own date with catastrophe. When I went through my recovery, I gravitated toward all the young soldiers who had come to the hospital with wounds similar to or more severe than mine. I drew strength in knowing we were going through the fire together.

In these pages, you will read testimonies of true survivors. Their courage is meant to encourage you. It's a form of peer support. *If they can do it, maybe I can, too.* It's natural to seek their guidance. I still do it all the time. It reminds me of comedian George Carlin's take on self-help: "If you want self-help why would you read a book written by someone else? That is not self-help, that's help." If we're open to learning from others, we can find help in the most unlikely places—the missing pieces and scars of the wounded.

Let's begin by facing facts: We all need help. No one survives alone.

3

STEP 1:

FACE FACTS

◆

This terrible thing has happened. It can't be changed. So, *now* what? There's little point wishing you hadn't gotten into that car, or gotten the tumor, or been fired from that job. We must face some brutal facts of the here and now. It's normal to question, but you will never get a satisfactory answer, and you'll only waste time. The past is the past, and facts are facts.

During my time recovering from my landmine injuries, there was not a lot of coddling. Ever. The Israelis were so practical it hurt. A nurse wheeled me into a new room, showed me my bed and hospital fatigues, and pointed to where to get lunch. *The dining hall? With the other inmates?* The attitude there was very *suck it up; fend for yourself*. It wasn't exactly a psych ward, but to small-town me, it seemed like a scene from the movie *One Flew Over the Cuckoo's Nest*.

At first I definitely did not appreciate the "you do it" attitude. *Hello? Do you not see the bloody stump here, people?* I remember having to wheel myself down to the lunch hall. No more breakfast-in-bed hospital rooms. All of these people start introducing themselves, practicing their English in the most uncomfortable way. They're all missing arms and legs, or eyes, or they're burned. I remember this older guy, in particular, who had been in the hospital for months going through rehab. He had a spanking-new above-the-knee prosthesis, and he tells me, "Don't worry, you'll have your own fake leg one day." He then took off his shiny leg, proudly revealing a big hairy stump.

That was the first stump I remember meeting. I hated looking at it. I wasn't even mildly intrigued by the thought of seeing this man's robotic parts. I wasn't ready. Among the group, I felt terribly alone in this world of disfigurement. Nothing in twenty years had prepared me for this. But I stayed. And I did get used to stumps and burns and mangled bodies. And what I learned—viscerally—was that we are more than our bodies. We laughed and made jokes and snuck out of the hospital. These guys were my friends and they got me through. We got each other through.

The hospital gave me no choice but to Face Facts: I was now an amputee. I had nearly six months in rehab to face it and to get to know my own stump. This is my new body, deal with it. I came to appreciate my stump—it was conical and clean, with an eight-inch scar where my remnant leg is sewn shut. Every orthopedic surgeon who has seen it since says, "Nice one. I'd be proud to have done that." As stumps go, mine is great. Thank you, Dr. Steinbach (my surgeon).

They were six formative months. If the staff had been too sympathetic or pitying, I would probably have sunk into a funk. Instead, I was visited by other amputees long out of the hospital who basically told me, "You have a nose cold, get over it." And so I did. Since my left leg had also been blown open, I couldn't rely on it for months. I had bone fragments that still had to be plucked out and shrapnel that had to be removed—and then there were the skin grafts. These were the facts, and I had to face them every day.

It wasn't an easy thing. There were many setbacks—infections, a troublesome wound here and there, pressure sores. The Israeli military physical therapists kept me active. I was too proud to say I was nervous when they yanked the wheelchair from me for good. And, again, when they started whipping a heavy green medicine ball at me while I stood on one leg in front of the mirror. They worked me beyond exhaustion. They had a plan for me, and my job was to get with the program. The routine was an inflexible fact. I drew on willpower I didn't know I had.

When something bad happens, threatening our very being and way of life, we feel the need to get rid of it, to somehow dispense with the negative experience as quickly as possible. There's an urge to clean up and move on, erasing evidence of the trauma. I know rape survivors who shower repeatedly to wash away the violation. I know war-injured people who drink to numb the memories. I know individuals in wheelchairs still praying to walk. This is natural. But aging and illness and death remain the constants of the human experience. Best to look at them, acknowledge them, and find a way to live with them. As the author James Baldwin puts it, "Not everything that is faced can be changed, but nothing can be changed until it is faced."

Emotions are facts, too. But it is quite common to deny the initial experience. *This is not happening to me. I will wake up from this nightmare soon.* It is also quite common to feel the most intense range of emotions after a loss or crisis. Listen to survivors across the world who have relayed to me in various languages the following sentiments to describe their reactions to loss:

Denial. *"This is no big deal." "Everything is fine." "I'll just wake up and none of this will have really happened."*

Revulsion. *"When I look at my body and think about what happened, I feel sick to my stomach." "I am disgusting. No one will want to look at me again."*

Fear and Anxiety. *"I won't be able to support my family now." "I don't want to spend the rest of my life in a chair." "What if I die?" "What if my spouse leaves me?"*

Guilt and Shame. *"Why is God punishing me?" "I must have done something to cause this." "I feel so embarrassed I can't tell anyone."*

Anger and Resentment. *"Someone's going to pay for this—it's not my fault." "Easy for them to say, they haven't been through anything like this." "What happened to me is WRONG!"*

Frustration and Helplessness. *"It takes me so long to do everything!" "Why don't people know how to help me?" "I cannot do anything now. I can't even dress myself anymore."*

Depression and Hopelessness. *"Nothing matters anymore." "My family would be better off without me." "I don't want to do anything. I just want to sleep." "I can't stop crying."*

So *say* it—whatever negative, self-pitying comments are rattling around inside your head. It is not helpful to pretend these feelings aren't real. It is best to deal with all of it neutrally, to lay them on the table as "facts." They need to be sorted through or they will reinforce one another in a spiral of despair. Denied or indulged in for too long, these emotions will plunge you into victimhood.

Everyone associated with an experience will have their own emotions and version of events. My mother, for example, says she lost a piece of her herself when I lost a limb. She kept asking to see and touch my wounds, as if to jolt her out of shock.

> There is a numbness that sets in when you do not want to feel. I carried that with me to Israel. But nothing could shield me from the shock of entering your hospital room. My holding you as tight as I could. "Do you want to see my leg?" (Yes, my dear son, let me see your hurts . . . Ah, Jerry, the foot is not there. IT IS GONE!) I did not say that out loud . . . I wanted to see your other leg, and your face, and where the doctors took the skin graft.

She had heard I'd lost a leg. But seeing the missing piece was entirely different—nothing under the sheet. Maybe she could disguise her shock, numb her pain, wish it all away somehow. It turns out that some denial or suppression of emotion can help in the immediacy of crisis as long as these short-term survival techniques aren't permitted to take hold. My mother says that at first she couldn't fathom that she had given me two feet at birth, and now one was gone. It was devastating to her emotionally. So she had to give herself time to adjust, and this meant recognizing the fact of denial—the temptation to think this will all be over soon; we can make it better. One friend came to visit me in the hospital and actually said he believed my missing limb would grow back!

Self-pity is another normal reaction to tragedy—a fact for us to face. *Why me? I don't deserve this!* Self-pity becomes dangerous if we don't recognize it for what it is—a natural human reaction to injury and injustice—and head it off at the pass. Emergencies trigger self-centeredness by necessity. Each of us must do what we can to survive, regardless of anyone else. But this self-involvement, when it extends well beyond the emergency phase, can turn into more destructive self-pity.

People need to nurse their wounds to some extent, and I don't blame them. I confess, it took me almost two years until I could accept that my right leg was decidedly gone, that my stump and scars were permanent. I was never going to ski on two legs again. From now on I would have to hop or crawl to the bathroom at night.

For me, the key to preventing self-pity was outing it. I learned to note the moments when I started to take account of what I "deserved." Emotions are as real as open wounds and as tough as old battle scars. I have come to see strong feelings such as self-pity and anger as things to name and to face. Invite the emotion out in the open to gain perspective and understand its place in the scheme of things.

It's one thing to feel sorry for ourselves. But when self-pity grows, it turns into narcissism. Resentment of others' blessings, particularly your friends and relatives—your own tribe—is a sure sign that self-pity has taken hold and that you are slipping into victimhood. It is common in twelve-step programs such as Alcoholics Anonymous (AA) for peers to allow only five minutes on the "pity pot." If someone is carrying on at a meeting, someone normally will intervene with a rebuke. "Yeah, yeah, we've all been there. It's time to move on and stop feeling so sorry for yourself. Your time is up!" Spoken like a seasoned survivor who understands what's at stake.

I think back to the big pains I've experienced: the mine-field, my parents' divorce, the suicide of a friend in rehab, the sudden death of others. I had to face the facts: "I will bleed to death if we don't get out of here." "My father and mother must live their own lives; it is not mine to fix." "I was lucky to have known Phil even for the short time I did." Wishing it all to go away is natural, but denial of facts is ultimately destructive.

My mother reflected on my accident years later.

When a tragedy happens to one you love, acceptance is not the first thing that happens in your heart. Denial is. When it dawns on you that this situation is unfixable, the rage and the depression and despair walk hand in hand. Betrayal of "the Universe" or of "God" is the next line of defense, and then blaming. Blaming Israel for not cleaning up their minefields and of course blaming God for not caring for me, my family and, of course, Jerry. Self-pity hangs around for a long time. Wanting to get pity for "all that I have suffered." That goes on a long time. When acceptance comes, it is a great freedom, and for me it was helped by watching the recovery of you, Jerry. If your recovery had not happened and your attitude was different, it might have been different for me.

Acceptance is not just for your benefit but for your loved ones, too. I think of several mothers and would-be mothers I know who have demonstrated remarkable capacity over the years to face facts. Why? There is generosity in coming to terms with personal pain so that it won't hurt others as well. Women often find resilience by committing to the welfare of others, not just themselves. Whether struggling with infertility, or stillbirth, or the death of an adult child, there are facts all around us—people who need and rely on us to be strong.

Carrie, a classmate from Michigan business school, has dreamed her whole life of having children. Now into her thirties, she is struggling with unexplained infertility. She is trying to come to grips with the diagnosis—not just to find her own peace, but also for the benefit of her marriage and her work life, running a family business.

I had my children's names picked out by the time I was a teenager. I even argued with my husband, prior to marrying, about the number of children we would have. I never dreamed I would have any trouble in the child-making department. After our wedding we decided to wait a few years so I could obtain my MBA without children in the mix. Today, the reality has set in. My husband and I have been trying to conceive for three years. We've been poked and prodded, questioned and analyzed, medicated and diet restricted. After years of tests we've been told we have "unexplainable infertility." Our tests are normal and we are healthy . . . yet something is not right. I have feelings of failure, sadness, and anger all wrapped in one.

But I've resolved myself to accept this reality and have faith in the future. To cope with my situation I talk with friends, enmesh myself in activities and groups, pray, exercise, and consider my options. The beauty of life is that we have options and choices. We can either choose to look at the glass half-empty or look at it as half-full. We can live as a victim of circumstances or we can accept reality and take action to do something constructive with it. I have many gifts that I need to focus on rather than focusing on what I don't have. Maybe God has a different plan for me.

Carrie will insist that her own personal struggle doesn't rank "up there" as a trauma, per se, but it has been a big challenge for her. We all wrestle with the facts of our lives, big and small, in order to find meaning as we strive to keep hope alive. Without coming to grips with what is happening, no matter how disappointing, we can't rethink our circumstances and then make room for new possibilities. Trying to ignore the pain is natural, even necessary at times, but avoidance can delay our ability to cope and move on.

Moving forward for the sake of the family is the unselfish goal of a mother I deeply admire. When she was six months pregnant, Elizabeth and her husband learned that their baby had a serious heart condition. Three months later the baby died in the womb, a few days before he was due to be born. At his birth, when she could finally see her first child, he was what the hospital termed "fetal wastage."

> Although the hospital staff was very supportive, putting me in a separate ward away from all the happy mothers and their new babies, it was difficult to know my child was in the morgue. I jumped at the chance the funeral parlor offered to have Joseph come to our home. I needed that time to know him and to feel like a mother. I needed to sit with him, to hold him, to show him the room we had decorated. I had to look at him and to touch him to be able to come to terms with the fact that he was dead. Then I could accept it. I could dress him in the clothes friends had sent with so much love and say goodbye. Then I could move forward.

There is no right way to grieve. Elizabeth did what she needed to do. And it opened the way for a future with a family.

Within a few years, Elizabeth had celebrated the arrivals of a healthy son and then twin daughters.

For parents, there is nothing more painful than the death of their child. On January 3, 2006, a talented young musician, Omri, was hit by an unlicensed drunk driver near his apartment in Brooklyn. His mother, Irit, flew from Tel Aviv and, immediately upon arrival at the hospital, showed her strength as a mother-survivor. She wanted all the facts. The police reports, Omri's friends' reconstruction of the accident. Exactly what had happened to her son? Who was with him? What was the expression on his face right before the car suddenly struck him?—seemingly mundane things that helped her understand exactly what had happened. I stayed with Irit at the hospital as she spent hours with her son while he was brain-dead but on life support, as the doctors prepared for his organs to be donated. Each time she stroked his foot, his toes would curl or his leg would twitch. *Was he still alive?*

Again and again, Irit had to pull aside the nurse or organ donor network coordinator to ask whether they were sure Omri was clinically dead. How did they know? *Is this nightmare real? In the morning, will I really have to give doctors permission to take out my son's heart?* I could only hold her hand as she went through this agonizing process of brutally facing the facts. After hourly consultations with her husband, Avi, back in Israel, discussing the facts as they became available, Omri's parents made the decision. Their son was technically dead—being kept alive by machines. It was time to release him and honor her son's wishes that his organs live on to help others.

How do mothers do it? Is it an ingrained habit of focusing on the needs of others first? The way Irit navigated the Victims Unit at Bellevue Hospital, even with English as her second language, was remarkable. She was acutely focused on what her son required, even lying there on a respirator. She told me,

> Jerry, I am a very practical person. I knew from the first phone call that Omri was dead in the brain and wouldn't recover. I'm here to do the hardest thing. I know Omri wouldn't want to live this way. This is not about me as a mother. It's about him. He's my son, and I will do the right thing for him, just like I always have since the day he was born.

One rarely sees such clearheaded analysis at the moment of shock. Usually, people dissolve in a puddle of emotion or retreat into denial or escape. We often hear of the two classic human responses to threat—flight or fight. Irit rationally avoided both. Instead, she stared at the facts before her, leaned on her husband, family and friends, and then took responsibility for what needed to be done.

Facing facts is one way we are able to break through denial and allow grief to do its work. We must repeat the facts to ourselves, letting them sink in. That's one of the reasons we Irish Catholics have a tradition of open-casket wakes. Though it makes the uninitiated cringe, there is nothing quite like a corpse to eliminate denial. During the funerals of my grandparents, great-aunts, great-uncles, and later, my own father, it was important for me personally to see the corpse. It's not a tradition for everyone, mind you, just helpful for some of us who, when faced with tragic news, need to see it to believe it.

After the worst happens, the two most common psychological responses are known as *intrusion* and *avoidance*. Intrusion involves suddenly reliving a traumatic experience, and can include nightmares and flashbacks. It's as if the experience is saying, "I am not going away until you face me." The facts intrude inconveniently, whether we want them to or not. We are forced to deal with an intrusive experience, to sort through our new reality and perceptions of the world.

Upon my return home from the hospital in Israel, I struggled to make sense of my new environment. The first time I walked across my backyard and through the woods to a neighbor's house, I started to sweat. I felt acute spikes of anxiety, and my heart raced. I didn't want to listen to the warnings in my head: *This is how it happens, Jerry. A sunny day. Blue sky. Watch your step. Life explodes.* I had to coach my brain to relax and recalculate what was a real threat and what wasn't. *This is Massachusetts, Jerry, there are no landmines here.* Even something as simple as standing at an intersection in Boston, waiting to cross the street, would trigger anxiety. *You could lose your balance any second. Stumble. Get hit by a bus.* I'm not sure any of my friends noticed, but for months I would always stand a few feet back from the curb, letting others cross the street ahead of me.

David, who helped carry me out of the minefield, also experienced heightened stress: "For weeks my legs would shake when I walked on grass. That event left a distrust of something good and beautiful due to the association it now had with man's evil desire to hurt and kill another." Now married, a father and doctor in Corpus Christi, Texas, David describes something inside that forces him to focus in the midst of a life-and-death crisis.

> You once told me you thought I had yelled at you in the minefield. I really don't recall that, and am a little shocked, as I'm sure you were at the time. Oddly enough, a few years earlier, I do remember yelling at my father as he lay dying

when he and I were alone at home and he had a heart attack. His breathing was agonal and his skin cyanotic as he lay near death. I was in high school and had had no medical or first aid training. After calling the operator to alert an ambulance (pre-911), I hovered over my father's body and told him I thought he was tougher than that and could hang on until help arrived. I swear JFK's story of PT-109 came to mind during that instant when he challenged his remaining crew to survive as they floated, waiting for rescue after their boat sank. That's a strange recollection, but today when shit hits the fan in the ER or I find myself in a critical situation with a person who is in a life-or-death dilemma, I often feel a surge of anger that sharpens my focus and brings my mind and body to bear totally on the situation.

Recent studies in neuroscience indicate there is a rush of adrenaline that gets triggered by an emergency with acute stress. A boost in testosterone, in both men and women, helps an individual focus better under extreme pressure. This clear focus on the facts of danger can be key to our survival.

Talking through what has happened also helps integrate the experience into a life perspective. One thing I have learned to help survivors decompress is to let them talk about it, in their own words, in their own way. Sometimes this needs to happen over and over. Repetition is part of accepting and assimilating facts, trying to get the memory straight. The Vietnam veterans who did not suffer post-traumatic stress disorder (PTSD) were generally the ones who stayed very connected to family and friends and did not shy away from bearing witness to their battlefield experiences, often repeating the stories in detail. They weren't afraid to face facts.

That's why when working with war victims, I try to create

opportunities for individuals to recount their experiences. I always look for the survivor narrative behind the victim story. In other words, I don't focus so much on the plotline and gory details of victimization. Instead, I ask, What made it possible for this person to survive? Where did they find their strength? How on earth did they endure? Searching for the resilience factors helps bring out the inner survivor, rather than just inviting a victim's tale of woe.

Avoidance—the repression of painful memories—is the other coping device we use in the face of disaster. We deploy the following tricks to help us look away from the facts:

- actively avoiding related thoughts and memories
- forgetting important aspects of what happened
- numbing ourselves, shutting down emotionally
- detaching emotionally from our environment

Sally was twenty-eight years old with one child and pregnant with another when she had a terrible car accident in 1978 in Australia. After her sixth surgery, she woke up heavily sedated to bad news: she had not only lost her leg, she had miscarried. Sally credits her "stubbornness" for keeping her alive and fighting.

> When I found out that my leg would have to be amputated, I felt nothing really, probably because of all the drugs. I remember feeling sorry for family and friends because they were so angry and upset. But I really felt nothing. As time went on, and operation after operation continued, I became annoyed. Annoyed that my life had changed, annoyed that part of my body had gone. I used to dream that one day soon it would grow back.

I decided from the start that I wouldn't participate in the hospital therapy, exercises, and mental help. I wanted to do it all myself, by myself—stubbornness! For about eighteen months I was stuck in a wheelchair (apparently never to be able to walk again, on the left leg that was so badly injured), and I needed my left leg to help me get up and do most of the work for the right leg that was still in the process of being operated on, so no artificial limb could be fitted for a while. At this stage, I couldn't even stand the pain of having the weight of a bedsheet on my ankle, so putting any weight at all on it was unthinkable.

One day at lunchtime, I was watching a TV show where a guest was talking about positive thinking, saying that if you really wanted to do something, then set your mind on it now, and just do it. Well, I decided then and there that I would stand on my left foot, and never let it give up, and I did!

Sally's denial and avoidance came to an end because of a moment watching a TV show.

Sometimes the moment of truth takes much longer. This was the case for my Iraqi friend, Zainab. It took years for her to put an end to her denial and disassociation. She grew up in Iraq as the daughter of Saddam Hussein's pilot. Her family lived close to the inner circle of power in the shadows of dictatorship. Zainab says she spent years suppressing the facts of her life. But the more she tried to move on from the past, the more it seemed to cling to her. When she was twenty, she left Baghdad to marry a thirty-three-year-old Iraqi living in the United States, only to suffer at the hands of an abusive husband she later divorced.

Since childhood, Zainab's mother had always told her to

"erase from your memory" anything too scary, like the kidnapping and killing of others they knew in Saddam's employ. So Zainab only faced her facts a little at a time, as the pressure of hiding her history caused her to break down and reveal things she had never admitted to herself. Only after Saddam Hussein was captured in 2003 did the dam finally break. Zainab writes in her memoir:

> I wanted to make myself whole again. I wanted to come clean. I wanted to do my job without feeling like a hypocrite. But I had been afraid for so long I didn't know how to get rid of the layers of fear inside me. Because I had survived by hiding my past, even from myself, I had never really pieced together the story of my own life. Which of the things that had happened to me were causes, and which were effects?[1]

Zainab worked hard to forge a successful life in America, but she couldn't fully heal until she broke her silence and stopped denying her past. Finally, she experienced a nervous breakdown, telling a female paramedic, "Nothing is wrong. Everything is going right in my life. I just don't know how to stop crying."[2] Zainab tells me that writing about her experiences became a complete catharsis. "It felt like the heavy, dark stone in my chest finally passed through me; it's gone now," she says. "Taking the time to piece together my personal story and my family's history has given me new energy" to face the future with optimism and strength.

Trauma is fundamentally about a loss of control and loss of connection. Life has betrayed us. Facing the loss of our life as we once knew it does not take place without some initial denial and faltering steps.

Twenty-six-year-old Libby was out of town for a wedding when she learned Hurricane Katrina was bearing down on her home in New Orleans. She didn't think too much of it at the time, because there were hurricane scares nearly every year in New Orleans, and the deadliest storms tended to sweep to the east at the last minute. The hurricane hit on August 29.

> I returned to New Orleans just before Halloween. I half expected to see ghosts everywhere . . . Driving into the city was otherworldly. I arrived at night. There were no lights on in the streets, even the interstate ramps, and the scene illuminated by my headlights was grim and scary. There were collapsed buildings and abandoned cars heaped all over, and piles of stuff that was indistinguishable and that you were afraid to look at for long enough to figure out what it was. Everything had a layer of sediment, like the city had been destroyed decades ago and abandoned.
>
> Clearing out my apartment was a process of slowly amputating parts of my life that were no longer viable. My appearance, my choice of music and movies, my whole inner world became rather dark during those weeks, but not out of despair. It was more about touching the darker side of life, accepting it and then integrating it. If you are scared of the things that go bump in the night, you can either run from them, or you can become a thing that goes bump in the night yourself.

Libby felt the darkness of those days, but made a plan to leave the city she loved. She relocated to Washington, D.C., and found a new job. She knew enough about herself to seek meaningful work with a survivor mission. There was no going back, only forward.

Facing the facts of our situation, letting in the pain, is never easy. But it is necessary. One of my college roommates, Adam, describes how he and his family dealt with the shock of his sixteen-year-old brother's cancer diagnosis:

> I got a phone call from my parents giving me the news, and asking me to leave work immediately and come downtown. Peter was going in for surgery right away. I had to stop at the house and pick up items for him—clothes, toiletries, etc. I was in shock more than anything. I just couldn't believe it or get any kind of emotional handle on it. I remember saying to my parents, "This can't be happening to us. This happens to other people." It was surreal going through these very practical steps, driving downtown, picking up clothes, etc. I was fine on the surface, but in a disconnected state of mind.
>
> My reaction was strange, in retrospect. I never became upset or cried, but I remember feeling agitated much of the time, and I had a persistent pain in my chest right beneath my breastbone . . . Then about two weeks after the surgery, during an argument with my parents, I "broke" and the proverbial floodgates opened.
>
> I remember staggering around the house from room to room, sobbing uncontrollably, writhing in absolute agony on a couch, a chair, a bed. I don't know what the hell I was doing, but it just went on and on and on. At some point it stopped, and I noticed that the pain in my chest was gone. I had finally let myself feel the enormity of my fear and grief, and I remember a kind of lightness set in afterwards . . . the physical pain was released.

Cancer and other life-threatening illnesses are a crisis for the entire family, not just the patient. Intense and tumultuous emotions are bound to trigger physical reactions, from stomach pain to insomnia and loss of appetite. Our bodies will set off their own alarms, as in Adam's case, letting him know he needed to vent. The mind–body connection is undeniable.

A colleague I worked with for years, Karen, has battled cancer on and off since 1994. But she learned very early to discern the difference between facts and possibilities. She has been through the roller coaster of testing and guesswork. With the support of her husband, Vic, and close friends, Karen has made literally hundreds of visits to hospitals, doctors, and mind–body healing specialists.

> For me, I have to say the key was and continues to be just knowing it is possible to survive. When I was first diagnosed I didn't ask what my prognosis was. I didn't want to know. I did want to know if it was possible to live. They said it was. Then I wanted to know if it was possible to live a long time. They said it was. They would try to follow that up with statistics about how likely it would be to survive, and I would generally cut them off. All I needed to know was that it was possible. It wasn't that I didn't want to face facts. To me, a prognosis is not a fact. The way I saw it, nobody knew for sure what was going to happen, and as long as it was possible that I would live, I preferred to think that would be the case. It was funny to me that they wanted to manage expectations and not give you false hope, but they weren't afraid to give you false despair! That doesn't mean I wanted them to lie and tell me it was possible if it wasn't. I just wanted to know if it was possible.
>
> When the cancer came back, it was six months after Vic and I got married, and just shy of the three-year period when the doctor says, "I think you are going to be fine."

This time the tumor was inoperable, between my heart and my lungs. I was pretty scared because this time I didn't think it was possible to survive. I went to Johns Hopkins for a second opinion about treating the recurrence. After the consult was over and I was getting ready to leave, the doctor said, "Karen, you know you are not dying now, right?" That changed everything! He said while I could not be cured, it was possible to live with the disease for a long time. I walked out the door with two things: I am not dying now, and it is possible I will live a long time.

To me, Karen is an example of thriving, not just surviving. Her optimism, warmth, and determination are engines for life. After a series of alternative therapies—mind–body treatments, visualization exercises, acupuncture—not to mention more radiation and surgery, Karen now appears cancer-free. She tells me, with a smile, that she rarely gets a cold.

How can we use the facts that confront us with unpleasant truth to help us survive catastrophe? Facing facts is so hard because it demands that we come to grips with our worst fears. It means admitting what we really think about disability, deformity, and death—all scary stuff. Most of us would prefer to look away and carry on our merry way without thinking about these things. But without a closer look in the mirror, examining the wrinkles of our traumatized life, we can't make sound decisions, and then proceed to change and grow.

I met Nitin nearly ten years ago after he had completed his master's degree in Pittsburgh and launched his humanitarian career. It wasn't too long after his own before-and-after moment, January 18, 1997. He was settling into his new work as an aid worker in Rwanda when his team was held hostage and shot by insurgents. Three of his colleagues were killed in that attack. Nitin, the sole survivor, lost his leg, which had to be amputated above the knee to save his life.

One of the hardest things I have had to do is to look at myself in the mirror and accept myself as being different than I used to be. I had to give up how I saw myself, be open to how others saw me, and willing to reach out for help with ordinary activities like changing a lightbulb. I had to learn to be okay with who I was.

It wasn't my fault I got shot. But I had to face the fact that others wouldn't necessarily take care of me. Honestly, I'd much rather have someone else deal with the mess of insurance, co-payments, and all the paperwork and telephone calls that come with illness or disability. Unfortunately, I didn't see anybody else jumping up to deal with it, and so I had to step up to the plate. It wasn't just with insurance, it's with all facets of my life. If I don't aggressively attack my problems, they just get exacerbated until they're a mess.

Nitin moved from facing his worst fears to laughing about them:

My worst fear in life was losing a body part. Then it came true, and it wasn't so bad. Learning to walk again was my next worst fear. And then that wasn't so bad. Soon, I was dancing. In fact, I was in a bhangra troupe that did a performance at the French Embassy. Since I couldn't do all the moves the others could, we decided that two of the other guys would grab me and do this twirl, where my legs were lifted off the ground because of centrifugal force. During the dress rehearsal, as we were getting into position, I felt my prosthesis give. It started to fall off. There I was spinning in the air, and my leg is getting looser. All of a sudden, it went flying off into the audience—just as the French ambassador walked in. The director had a fit. The audience had a shock, and it was all I could do to prevent myself from laughing hysterically. I found when I faced my fears, I had the courage to laugh, and life wasn't so bad.

Facing fears, facing facts—the truth allows us to gain perspective. Maybe it's not as bad as we thought? Maybe we in fact can cope with this nightmare. Nitin points to a primary tenet of Buddhism and Hinduism: suffering in this life is universal and inevitable, but it is not an injustice. It is simply a lesson to help us reconfigure balance, overcome our weaknesses, and proceed to change and growth. Sometimes our "suffering results from our attachments to things and ideas, more than from the loss itself. Nitin had to let go of how he thought things would be, and examine how they really are. This is also what Libby had to do after becoming a Katrina refugee. She notes, "Life is not inherently less good because I no longer live in New Orleans after Katrina. My suffering comes from my attachment to the way I remember the city, and the 'me' I was in that life and thought I would always be."

In my own case, I was not rendered permanently unhappy when I lost my leg. I had lived with both legs for twenty years. Initially, I couldn't fathom missing one. It didn't sink in for some time that this was the new me—a one-legged hunk of burning love.

Before we can make the most of life after a drastic change, physical or otherwise, we must let go of the attachment to our old self-concept, and to a future we have banked on. None of it is permanent. We must face our disappointment and then be willing to redefine these things. It's a continual process. Lama Surya Das, a popular spiritual teacher and Tibetan Buddhist, writes:

> The first step in handling suffering is to look at our losses realistically. Put aside all illusions and delusions about what could have been or should have been. Then squarely face the grief and the pain. Acknowledge your tears and unhappiness. Know what you are experiencing. This is the opposite of denial. Feel it, examine it, and reflect upon it. Sense directly in the present moment how it affects you in your body and your mind.[3]

I certainly recommend this sensory approach to facing facts. But it's damn hard to do. Self-deception is a clever tool in the service of victimhood, and it conspires to keep us from properly seeing ourselves as we are, thereby interfering with what we need to do to mend our brokenness. Never underestimate the power of self-deception. But equally powerful is the truth that will set you free.

Great teachers and prophets admonish us to get real with ourselves, no matter how humiliating the facts. We are imperfect, and no matter how hard we try, we cannot fully control our lives. None of us will get very far without first examining our circumstances, relationships, and feelings. We will need to be ruthless in our self-assessment.

And when the time comes for us to decide how to respond to our new reality, will we get busy living or get busy dying? If we don't choose death, we must choose life.

4

STEP 2:

CHOOSE LIFE

◆

Crisis and pain can hold us hostage for a time, but we still have a choice in how we will respond to our circumstances, no matter how dire. When something disrupts our life, how do we move forward? I've seen it time and time again in my work with victims of war atrocities—there are those who fight for their lives after devastating loss and those who succumb to their suffering. Why the difference?

To truly thrive, we must *consciously choose* for our lives to go on in a positive way. I have had to do it more than once. Most of us have, or will.

We may feel like giving up, but few of us really want to roll over and *die*. We'd rather be Rip Van Winkle and wake up in one hundred years, after our crisis is long gone. In the end, we don't want to surrender to death; we just want this suffering to end.

Choosing life is akin to swinging between two monkey bars, letting go of one just as you reach for the second. It requires faith that the second bar will hold your weight. It can take all the inner strength you can muster to let go long enough to choose a new path out of your personal nightmare. But it is an endeavor that must be undertaken. Passivity is a killer. Choosing life requires a willingness to fight. Your mind, spirit, and body must all engage in this daily battle to align for life.

After my experience in the minefield, a common question was, "*Aren't you pissed, Jerry? Shouldn't someone pay for this?*" It's not that I didn't have my angry moments—especially in the beginning. But my expectation of *myself* was that I wouldn't go there. I didn't like that image of myself—bitter, whiny Jerry who let a bad thing take over the rest of his life. There is a life to be lived—my life—and if I had to hop, roll, or whatever, I was going to get back to it.

At first, getting out of bed each morning was a challenge. The alarm sounds. Get out of bed and wheel yourself to physical therapy at 7:30 A.M. Just get up. Or just get yourself to the park every day. Call friends and make plans even when you don't feel like it. Eventually it becomes easier, even habitual. A routine, little by little, will ensure progress, an opportunity to see light flicker at the end of the tunnel.

Are you willing to try? *Willingness* to be open to your future is crucial. Curiosity helps. In the depths of pain, we might ask ourselves, How much worse could this get? One reason we survive crisis is our hope and belief that this moment will change. *No, this is not the end.* Each minute is excruciating, but we have to stay in the game. The question is, What can I do now that the scourge is upon me? Alcoholics live O.D.A.T.—one day at a time—but in crisis we must survive O.M.A.T.—one moment at a time.

Death seems like an option—a *choice* in the midst of darkness. "I can choose to end this now." But is death really a choice? It's saying that our situation is larger than we are. My own choice to live is visceral. I'm driven to see what's over the next hill. Choosing life is also intellectual, in the sense that we must apply our minds to think differently about our moments of crisis. Don't just feel what's happening. Think about it; think past it. The threat comes when we believe a moment is larger than life. The key is to remember that life is larger than this moment. That is the perspective we must grasp.

Only by gaining perspective, by looking forward, by staying connected to life, can we move forward. We reclaim life. Not some noble, sad shell of a life, either. But a red-blooded, laughter- and tear-studded life that demands us to live it.

One of my friends talks about her suicide attempts before being diagnosed with bipolar manic depression and starting medication. She is clear about her hard-won decade-long battle for mental health:

> The darkest depression is like a tight chain that makes your whole emotional being smaller, limited and rigid. It is so narrow and tight, you feel like you cannot turn away. It is being stuck. There is no light in this hole. Sometimes I lived in the darkest suicidal depression and other times I soared to the highest of highs. And the common thread of this painful existence was a commitment to self-destruction.
>
> The craziest part was that through it all I functioned. Some force kept telling me, "There is another way." Day-to-day I was hanging on by the slightest thread. I had a million friends and always managed to earn money in interesting and meaningful jobs. I had a loving family. But every day was a little death that could not come soon enough. Pills, razors, and a flight of stairs were all strategies to make the pain go away.

At one point my psychotherapist said to me, "Be careful . . . in one of these suicide missions you might really hurt yourself." In retrospect, I believe my shrink was very effective at deferring the moment of suicide. "Wait another hour and call me."

When the pain is so intense that you choose to kill yourself, you do not want to choose life. You are not really choosing death, either . . . you just want the pain to go away. At the points that my shrink persuaded me to wait and call him back and then wait until the morning, I discovered that things do organically change and the impulse to destroy yourself is quieted. At those moments deep in the pit something usually small touches you. I went to therapy for an emergency session and the shrink had a can of diet Coke. I was babysitting at one point. The ten-month-old saw a funny toy and burst out laughing. Or the weather changed . . . It is those subtle moments—almost distractions—that energize you to look for a way out of the pits . . . Then step one is almost always asking for help.

Personally, I feel upset, even angry, when I think of my friend wanting to kill herself. I don't want to believe it, but it's a fact. It's her life, not mine, but I lose if she opts out of life prematurely. Her life has enriched mine enormously, and that of countless others. Apparently, I want her to live for selfish reasons. Why? So I can bask in her gifts and potential; so the world can benefit from her living, thriving. I believe the world can't afford the good dying young, before their time.

Everyone who embraces survivorship will be in a position to help others. It's a ripple effect—we touch many more lives than we imagine. Consider who would be affected for better or for worse if you were to die before your time. If you answer "no one," then you need to get professional help. I'm not being glib. It's a fact.

Studies on people who say they want to commit suicide, or have attempted to, reveal that we don't really want to *die*. Most of us fear death and the unknown. We really just want to *end the pain*, to be *released*, finally. But wouldn't it be better to be released into life?

I know survivors who didn't want to survive at first. Jesús Martinez in El Salvador was seventeen and living through civil war in 1989. He had a job in the city and had to take a bus to work. Because of roadblocks set up by guerrillas, he had to get off his bus, walk around the roadblock, and get on another bus to continue his journey to work. "I was a teenager, and not aware of the danger of mines. Everyone just got off the buses and walked on the side of the road. I don't know why I was walking where no one else was, but I remember someone saying there might be mines. I didn't think about it much." Walking along the side of the road, he stepped on a mine that blew off both his legs on the spot. The explosion was so powerful that others walking near him were wounded. He never lost consciousness, but he did lose hope.

> I fell in a hole. Both of my legs were blown off. I had blood in my mouth. My arm was wounded, and really, I thought it was all a bad dream. I tried to kill myself with an explosive that was lying on the ground near me. It didn't explode when I picked it up. When the soldiers arrived, I took a gun from one of them and begged him to kill me with it. I remember being so desperate to die, and saying over and over, "Please kill me."

Jesús did not die that day. He became a survivor.

The healing process was very difficult for me. There was the healing of my body, and also the trauma in my mind. I am thankful that I had the support of my family. It was very important for me to meet other disabled people, and see how they lived their lives. Sports had always been a part of my life, and I was very happy when I saw people practicing wheelchair sports in the hospital. It has been a long journey from wanting to die to getting where I am now. I am very happy and excited about many aspects of my life. I have a wife, my children, a family, my parents and siblings, and a very wide circle of friends.

My greatest satisfaction is knowing I can help others. It is surprising to see other survivors arrive in hospitals who are going through the same process I did. They are like me. They look at me, I talk to them, and they can see that I went through a similar experience and that I survived. Then the next time I visit with them, or I run into them, they are showing a completely different face. That joy is something that cannot be compared to anything. Wow. I am part of making another person happy.

Jesús learned to think of his circumstances differently. Again, what happens in the mind and heart is key to survival.

Your willpower and courage cannot be found in another person. There are people around us who give support, but we have to reach deep and dig up our own power for the struggle. Only *you* can make the choice to muscle through your present darkness. As British writer Gilbert Keith Chesterton warns, "Every man has his own courage, and is betrayed because he seeks in himself the courage of other persons."

This is a very important point. You *will not* find salvation in another person. You have to "work out your own salvation with fear and trembling," as Paul writes in his *Letter to the Philippians* (2:12) in the New Testament. *You* must choose life. You will find your own words in your own language to describe your journey forward.

I confess that for me, it was cursing and loud groaning. I'm not much of a sailor, but I did discover a string of favorite despicable words to blurt out. I wanted to let the darkness know how much I hated it, cursed it, every second of it. But I did not want it to defeat me. I wanted to live. (And secretly, I wanted others to know I was in *a lot* of pain.)

Pain is a wake-up call. It sends out warnings loud and clear. David is another one of us who was given a second chance at life. David used to be a clown with the Ringling Brothers, Barnum and Bailey Circus, but now makes a living as a business consultant and change management coach living in New Hampshire. He recounts a stark turning point on February 3, 1998, when intense pain concentrated his mind on what matters most: life and purpose.

> At the age of forty-two, on the first day of vacation in Lima, Peru, I collapsed with chest pains in the National Museum. One moment I am laughing about erotic pottery with my wife and planning my next day's hike to Machu Picchu, and the next thing I am scared beyond belief, grabbing my chest and sitting in a pool of my own vomit. I am medevaced to the United States, where I'm told I am an immediate candidate for quintuple bypass surgery. Seven major blockages, two at 90 percent. I was a day away from dead.
>
> Before surgery, I wandered a bit in life. There were lots of good times, but also a litany of comatose behaviors that often got me in trouble . . . My life was frequently complicated.

It's been nine years, and I am still working to integrate what *was* into what *is*. I am still working to understand the "bypass" of my own life. A few years ago I returned to Peru and climbed Machu Picchu. I went back to divinity school . . .

Heart surgery has given me this: the understanding that life is short, it can pass in a blink. And our dreams don't care if we are happy; our dreams only care that they are lived.

David tells me his goal is simple—to stay awake. That's a nice way to think about how to Choose Life. Stay tuned to what is happening around you and inside you. Mindfulness and consciousness are a discipline, much like getting out of bed in the morning to face the day.

Halfway across the world from David, Jacinta is a Mozambican woman I met through my work. Her husband was disabled from an injury during the civil war, trying to help a fellow soldier. They live in extreme poverty and her husband often has trouble finding work. But Jacinta sees their life as good, filled with love and laughter.

I am here living. We are missing a lot of things, yes, but we can live like that . . . He is able to do some things at least for a week, and he laughs here with us at home . . . I even tell him stories I hear in church so he doesn't feel so bad.

I will never send my husband away, as many have told me to do because of our poverty, because I believe one cannot buy love in the market. You cannot buy love with furniture or money. What belongs to love is love, and whatever this poverty is in our house, we are living according to our means with our three children here at home.

I like that thought: *What belongs to love is love*. You may be surrounded by poverty and want, but you can still expand your home tent hospitably to let in love, light, and laughter. Some days we go looking for them, and they seem to be hiding. We have to believe they will return. In this way, chosing life requires a seed of faith. The point of believing is to create options for the future. We hope by making this or that choice that we will open the door to bigger and better options ahead.

I used to think God was the one responsible for guaranteeing my future. So when I was injured, I struggled spiritually. I was hurt, feeling that God had fallen asleep at my wheel. I had to learn that God would not dole out special favors to spare His children from disaster. I also learned that God did not lessen my physical and emotional pain after each surgery just because I asked Him to. It turns out that this Creator was not a big gumball dispenser in the sky, activated by my two-quarter prayers. I began to understand that my fervent prayers, unanswered over time, were more about me venting my fears and anxiety than about securing miracles. Venting, it turns out, is very useful. It is a plea for empathy in the universe. *Please, someone out there, tell me you understand, dammit!* God wasn't my wishing genie—it was up to me to use whatever I had left to get on with my life.

The ability to Choose Life is a frame of mind, a decision that may be encouraged by faith and spirituality, but is certainly not dependent on a particular religious belief. What I have found is that the most resilient survivors I meet around the world agree that we are more than our bodies. Our circumstances and DNA don't fully define us. Spirituality can play a very important role in recovery, across all faiths, religions, and cultures.

I know many people of faith who don't see themselves as particularly religious or spiritual. Ross is a family friend and avid yachtsman. He has seen a lot during his seventy-odd years. He has had his share of trauma (starting with the death of his younger brother, Richard, from an aneurism at age thirteen, and soon thereafter a college roommate, and another close friend) and his share of triumphs (graduating from Princeton and crewing the first American entry in the Sydney–Hobart yacht race, breaking the course record). Then the wake-up call.

> Two years after Kathleen and I married, we were not having any luck making babies. Kathleen was diagnosed with ovarian cancer, fatal then and fatal today with only the rarest exception. Kathleen endured a tough operation and the torture of cobalt radiation that burns up your insides for forty-five days. I was a wreck. The wire of strength within all of us is incredibly strong but oh so thin, and when it breaks, one's world changes forever. We got through. She survived. Her terrific doctor went to bat for us so that we have two wonderful adopted kids, and now their wonderful spouses and grandkids.
>
> Most important, Kathleen's victory snapped me to attention. I knew in seconds as never before why I am here and who and what is important, Love, Sharing, Helping, Trust, Communication, Building Life as a Family, all the tenets of Friendship and spreading them out to others. Most important, us.
>
> Thinking of turning points in my life—so far, the crises are important! People who (appear to) go through life without the odd crisis will miss a great deal including the instant snap into focus of reasons for living, or even a slow progress toward it.
>
> *"La dicha es mucha en la lucha"*—"The reward is great in

the struggle." Set out and find it, especially if it does not find you.

Most of the time we don't have to look for it, because struggle will find us. That's a guarantee. And when it comes, it sure helps if we can maintain our perspective and a sense of humor. Life is diminished without laughter. Humor is one of the most important keys to choosing life—a way to see through our dark circumstances.

For many survivors emerging from years of sadness or depression after a deep loss, the hint that they might want to live again came in the form of an unexpected chuckle. *What was that? Wait, did I just laugh?* It might have been months or years since feeling that release in the belly. A mother told me once it was a full ten years after her son died before she remembered genuinely laughing at something. It surprised her so much that she figured it was the first indication that she might, in fact, want to live again.

Humor heals. Christopher Reeve recalled,

As the day of the operation drew closer, it became more and more painful and frightening to contemplate . . . I lay on my back, frozen, unable to avoid thinking the darkest thoughts. Then, at an especially bleak moment, the door flew open and in hurried a squat fellow with a blue scrub hat and a yellow surgical gown and glasses, speaking in a Russian accent. He announced that he was my proctologist, and that he had to examine me immediately. My first reaction was that either I was on way too many drugs or I was in fact brain damaged. But it was Robin Williams . . . and for the first time since my accident, I laughed.[1]

In Israel, there was one guy on the ward, probably in his fifties, who never laughed. He had recently lost his limb above the knee to diabetes and vascular disease. He seemed ages older than the rest of us, and no fun at all. At this point, most of my roommates were waking up off and on in the middle of the night with irregular attacks of phantom pain. Most of them would beg the nurse for sleeping pills or muscle relaxants. We'd unsympathetically tell one another to shut up. One night, this guy, I can't remember his name, responded to my joking asides by saying, "This isn't funny. Look at us. We can't sleep. We can't walk. What type of life is this?" He went dark on us. The room went quiet. I rolled over in my bed with a note to self: *Stay away from him. He's toxic to me.*

I have come to respect how ruthless we can and should be when it comes to our own recovery path. I know I was. Laughter is my way of choosing life, of releasing tension, of gaining perspective, even through the dark nights of hospitalization. I needed as much as I could get of that oxygen. If a person was distracting me from that imperative, I would just roll past him or her in my wheelchair. I couldn't have this person in my circle. *Stay away from the negative guy.* In a crisis, taking on others' depression can feel toxic, contagious, and somehow dangerous.

A friend of mine who struggles with manic depression credits her survival, at least in part, to humor.

In my years of depression, life was a crisis, but I hung in there for some reason. When people helped me laugh at myself that was always helpful. Most people were afraid of my black world, but some just helped me laugh and the laughter made me realize there was some choice.

You'd think MK, a young woman who stepped on a landmine while herding her family's cattle in Eritrea, would not
find too much to laugh at. But sometimes there's nothing quite
as silly as joking about our lowest common denominator: gas.
MK recounts, "In the hospital, there was a lady who would
slap anyone who farted in her presence. But whenever I did it,
she slapped the others—my visitors! I always burst into loud
laughter." MK describes how she loved to laugh, as it helped
her to keep some perspective and try to stay positive, even
through the dark days of homelessness after she was kicked
out of her uncle's house.

> The fact I had to leave my uncle's place was good for me. I
> would have idled away my time there, doing nothing. I
> could have never reached this stage in my life. So I know
> that even unfortunate incidents can change things for the
> better in one's life. When they denied me access to their
> house, it was good for me because I was able to make ac-
> quaintance with other people and start to progress in life.

Research indicates that just having a positive outlook like
MK can extend one's life.[2] Today, 93 percent of Americans believe that perceptions, thoughts, and choices affect physical
health.[3] Survivors in recovery can testify from experience that
a dose of hope and optimism will bring more healing than
gloom and pessimism. High levels of hostility are in fact better
predictors of heart disease than high cholesterol, cigarette
smoking, or obesity.[4]

We are waking up to the mind–body health connection. We
understand that the two are linked, but we are still more likely
to seek psychological help only when facing deep depression or
suicidal thoughts. People are proactive in treating their physical

wounds, but disappointingly passive when it comes to dealing with the mental struggles associated with life's ups and downs.

One of my wife's closest friends since childhood, Chrissy, is a kickass practical person. She's a gifted athlete and a generous friend. She never overdramatizes but does find humor in life. Except for that miserable year after her husband left her. "The jerk," we called him. He walked out only days after Chrissy had knee surgery and they had moved into a new condo. It turned out her husband had just completed parole. She had told no one, not even her closest friends, as she worked faithfully to keep her "jerk" out of jail in a failed attempt to save the marriage. Chrissy remembers the first few months without her spouse:

> I would wake up every morning, and the television was still on from the night before. It would stay on until I went to work. I'd come home from work and lie in bed, turn it back on, and stay there until I fell asleep. I did that for a long time. I finally got mad at myself and thought, "What a loser!" And that's when I started to come back.

She refused to accept defeat and began to rebuild. It meant going to daily physical therapy to get her knee back in shape, while getting her condo furnished and unpacked. She didn't *feel* like doing any of it, but she believed she had a different future ahead. She hoped for a different future, anyway. Chrissy decided to buy her ex out of the condo and make it *her* home, decorated just the way *she* would like it.

> I wasn't going to let this person, who I had protected and helped, get the best of me. My "revenge" was to pick up the pace of living and find some fun. Sure, it meant a lot of

weekends partying at the beach with a tad too much drinking and dancing, and then working like a madwoman during the week, but I got through it. I swung like a pendulum, but then found myself again. After about a year of this, I was able to let go of the marriage, of him, of what was meant to be, but wasn't. I would take responsibility for my own life going forward.

True to her survivor instinct, Chrissy refuses to accept defeat. She starts over. Today she is remarried and has a spunky daughter, much like her mom.

I remember reaching my lowest emotional point in a hospital bed the day after major surgery to cut though another piece of bone. I was physically and emotionally exhausted. Two friends from Jerusalem were sitting by my bedside, but I was feeling absolutely and utterly distraught and alone. I didn't think I could take this pain for another moment. I began to sob uncontrollably. My heart and brain were at a breaking point. It felt as if someone were sitting on my head and chest, suffocating me. *I can't take another second.* The next second comes and goes. *I'm serious, I can't take even one more moment.* Then another moment passes me by. This went on and on. Finally, I realized I had a choice: live or die. I chose to live.

My high school friend Kate suffered for years from anorexia. Looking back, she remembers, "I realized I was killing myself slowly." When I had visited her in the hospital, she confessed through tears, "I don't want to die." But she was already at death's door, her skeletal body shutting down, exhausted from years of punishment. I told her, "I can't help you. What am I going to do? Tie you up and feed you oatmeal? *You* have to do it. No one can force you to get better." Kate chose to climb out. Thank God it wasn't too late. She channeled her formidable willpower to live, relearning to care for and feed herself. No one could do it for her. Not her friends, her mom, not even God. Kate bore the responsibility. She is now a nurse, successful manager, and mother.

How do we, like Kate, turn things around? The American Psychological Association says it's a mental rather than physical battle. We build our resilience mentally by:

- nurturing a positive view of ourselves
- keeping things in perspective
- maintaining a hopeful outlook

Dragana, who lives a continent and ocean away from Kate, in Bosnia-Herzegovina, learned to master all three.

I was waiting in my doctor's office. I did not realize the words I was to hear next would cause me to feel a chill like I had never felt before.

"'I am sorry to give you the bad news, but you have cervical cancer."

I felt numb and voiceless. The only thing connecting me to the reality of that moment was a bad headache I instantly got. In disbelief, I simply could not take in the full meaning of what she was saying. I felt nothing. Just emptiness. I have no idea how long I was sitting in silence or what happened next. I switched onto my autopilot and we "calmly" agreed to the next steps, biopsy, surgery. When I stepped out into the cold, I felt so, so alone. A million questions were racing through my mind: Why? How will I tell my parents? Will it hurt? Will I live? Can it be possible? My throat was aching with suffocated tears. I felt that something was taking away the sense of control over my life.

I cried. The crying was good. I needed to release the tension in order to start thinking straight. While I was calming down and regaining composure, I tried to recall all those things I was brought up to believe: "Regardless of the situation, I have a choice." "Do not be afraid, or let fear humiliate you." "Distinguish the things that are under your control and influence." "Do not give up before you even try to fight," and "Try hard!" As I talked to myself, the meaning of this "thing," the cancer, a threat to me, started to change and take the shape of an opponent—a life test that I had to and wanted to resolve.

I know it sounds like a contradiction, but I believe that the hardest tests and losses I have lived through have made me a richer and, in many ways, better person.

Dragana is a role model for thriving. She decided to take charge of her own life, not only to choose it but to fight for it. What a difference a decision makes. What a difference her mind-set made. I hear from many survivors like Dragana who became thrivers when they *decided* to live. Even with friends who eventually succumbed to death, there was nobility in their fight to the end. They did not *go softly into that dark night.* That was their life's choice.

The most resilient among us seem to benefit from an internal moral compass such as fighting for your country or surviving for the sake of your children. Having a purpose can strengthen a survivor's feeling of self-control, the sense of being in the driver's seat. It's okay if you feel a tad superior to victims and victimizers sinking around you. You must cheerlead yourself forward.

I think of Margaret in northern Uganda, who was riding the bus a few days before Christmas in 1998, when it drove over an antitank mine and was attacked by guerrillas.

We heard gunshots and knew we were in an ambush. Everyone went wild. When I tried to run, I noticed one leg came out and the other, there was no shoe, no leg, and there was a very ugly thing I was looking at, not my leg, but something with the flesh hanging. But my mind was still, "Huh? What happened to my leg?" So I started to hop, and I lowered myself to the grass and tried to crawl. It was the dry season, so the grass was very high and dry and thick. So this hanging flesh kept getting caught, until I just gave up, and laid still.

That's when the soldier came. I closed my eyes, but I could feel his presence. And the next thing, he started to undress me. I was wearing jeans. And I thought, "Now, what does he want?" Normally, the rebels, they want clothing. And I had on a jacket and trousers. But there were also stories of how they abuse. And that's when I started praying. And then my trousers got stuck, and he's yanking on them, and going through my pockets.

All through, I kept my eyes closed. I would hold my breath, so he could not see me breathe. Then he shot me. I think he wanted to know if I was still alive. And I just kept still. So he just flung me, and I fell where he threw me. He shook me four times, threw me this way and that way, this way and that. And then he hit my leg with the gun, very hard. The pain wasn't so much. But I did feel pain, and was sweating. And he had seen the sweat, but when I didn't move, when I didn't say a word, I never opened my eyes, and I heard his footsteps walking away. This all happened in about five minutes.

About an hour later, the government soldiers came. And when I crawled out and saw all these guns pointed at

me, one of them said, "Are you a rebel?" I said, "No. Are
you the army?" He said yes. I crawled to him and I grabbed
his leg and I wouldn't let go. Two other soldiers tried to pry
me off, but they couldn't. Finally he said, "Let go so we can
help you." And they took me to the hospital . . . I knew I
had to live . . . I kept thinking of my babies.

When she first told me her story, I was stunned. Can you
imagine the strength needed to play dead? Margaret, a single
mother, didn't budge for the sake of her five kids who needed
her to live.

Will you choose a future? For your own sake, as well as for
your family?

Historic and literary figures alike grasp what's at stake: a
life-and-death battle for our minds and hearts. "Sometimes
even to live is an act of courage," writes poet Carl Sanburg in
the twentieth century, echoing eighteenth-century Italian play-
wright Conte Vittorio Alfeieri: "Often the test of courage is
not to die but to live." Why not give the new day a chance?
How much worse can this get? That's what we ask when we want
to convince ourselves to keep the door open. After all, why
give up a minute before the miracle? You just might discover a
flicker of hope, even as the abyss of despair mocks the
thought. Harriet Beecher Stowe counseled, "Never give up,
for that is just the place and time that the tide will turn."

By choosing life we step across the second threshold of
survivorship. It may be one of the hardest steps. It requires
imagination and perspective in the midst of pain. It comes on
the heels of brutal facts and a long look in the mirror to see
who we are and where we stand. How do you choose your
way forward with scars and bitter memories? You don't let

your situation define you. You reframe how to think about it. You choose humor and connections and love—you choose to live.

One of the essential ways we start to embrace life is by reaching out to others.

5

STEP 3:

REACH OUT

◆

No one survives on their own, and no one thrives alone, either. Yes, you might feel an excruciating loneliness after one of life's hurtful blows. But we are simply not built to survive solo. Isolation will kill us, not protect us. We humans are social animals made for community. Even when family and friends annoy the hell out of us, they remain an essential part of our survivorship.

One must find peers, friends, and family to break the isolation and loneliness that come in the aftermath of crisis. We have to let the people in our life *into* our life. In our hour of need, we may even depend on the grace of mere acquaintances or total strangers. Some will surprise us, coming out of the woodwork to help. Others—very often our best buddies and closest siblings—will disappoint us terribly.

I often told myself during points of crisis when I felt tempted to isolate, "Dammit, just make a call to someone . . ." To survive, we must find empathetic souls—sympathetic surrogates. Our inner *victim* may shun this, preferring to retreat into a shell. However, our inner *survivor* craves people. We need to find people who understand what we are going through. Social support is absolutely essential.

I have never been a big believer in the "self-made man." We all live off previous generations, combined gene pools, and preexisting social networks. We have benefited from anyone and everyone who has ever been kind to us, encouraged us, taught us, mentored us, or parented us.

Still, when you are in a deep, dark, relentless pit of pain, it's hard to think of others. But make no mistake about it, they are there. Others are in the room with you, in the wings of the hospital with you, in prayer for you, in kitchens cooking for you, on cell phones spreading the word on your behalf. In trauma, you may have become the lead character, but there is an ensemble cast of participants and a host of witnesses. How you keep the door open to relationships will determine the extent to which you are able to thrive years later.

I benefited greatly from social support while in Israel. Frankly, if you're going to step on a landmine, you might *want* to do it there, where trauma is sadly normal. You'll find a lot of peers and families who have known your suffering—they've been there. And when you share a hospital room with others in the same predicament, you don't have a lot of time to brood alone.

In the hospital, I shared a room with "guys like me." Hundreds were getting blown up in Lebanon at the time. If I'd come back to the States I would have had plenty of great friends and family, but no one who had experienced war injuries. Back in Boston, it was difficult for my relatives to understand; few people were thinking about war and terrorism, let alone minefields. In Israel I was normal. I had peers and we supported each other. It was another key to recovery.

Friends and classmates from my studies at Hebrew University heard about my accident and many made the three-hour pilgrimage repeatedly, taking two or three buses from Jerusalem to the hospital in Safed. My room was an open-door party place of sorts. They'd bring guitars and cookies and music. The atmosphere was so Israeli casual that friends even slept on spare hospital beds. I suspect they wouldn't have allowed that at Mass General in Boston.

With so many people coming and going, it was clear that social support—a primary ingredient for overcoming crises—was not missing from my life. Perhaps I was spoiled with too much, if there can be such a thing. There were days when I was exhausted by support . . . I didn't want to have everyone and his uncle pouring through to gawk or make small talk with me. But still, too much is better than not enough (if you have to choose). I certainly can't complain.

Fritz and David remained my core support, changing bedpans and urine bottles on demand, washing me, shaving me, helping to deal with the basics, while still keeping their sense of humor as I yelled each time they knocked the bed without warning, triggering new ripples of pain. I also recall fondly the blond nurses on missions from Denmark—Krista, Anne, Hannah, Irene—saintly beings who brought light (and shortbread cookies) with each visit. My Jerusalem classmates brought comfort food, good humor, and music, including Ray, who played guitar and sang the same hymns again and again, at my insistence.

A few weeks after my accident, an Israeli stranger paid me a visit—an extraordinary moment in which another survivor reached out to me. He walked up to my bed and said that he, too, had stepped on a landmine, but in Lebanon. "Can you tell which leg I lost?" He was wearing blue jeans and walked with a perfect and steady gait back and forth in front of my bed. Was he showing off? Was I in the mood for this game? "I can't tell." I really couldn't. "That's my point," he said. "The battle is not down there, but inside you, in here and up here," pointing to his heart and then to his head. "By the way, do you still have your knee?" Yes. "Can you still have kids?" I think so; yes, it still works. "Then what you have is a nose cold. You'll get over it."

He turned and walked out of my room as steadily as he entered. I never met him again, and to this day I don't remember his name. But I'll always remember that visit, that moment. It posed a choice, a mental fork in the road. I thought to myself, *If this Israeli guy can do it, I certainly can.* Maybe I'd be okay in the end. Maybe I would be able to walk and then run and swim and play tennis again. Women would still be attracted to me. Maybe I'd eventually start a family. It dawned on me that losing my leg wasn't the same as losing my life.

I believe this provocative peer visit was the beginning of reclaiming my power. Just as Albert Schweitzer describes, "At times our own light goes out and is rekindled by a spark from another person. Each of us has cause to think with deep gratitude of those who have lighted the flame within us." Well, if you're out there, my anonymous amputee visitor, *shalom vey todah hevri*—"Peace and thank you, my friend."

Looking back, I am so grateful for my eclectic collection of friends. Before the accident, I had spent months in Israel reaching out to strangers and making new acquaintances across the land—Christians, Muslims, and Jews alike. I had determined that my junior year abroad would serve as an out-of-my-comfort-zone opportunity to meet a range of characters. By the time I stepped on a landmine, I'd created a diverse network of friends and acquaintances that extended broadly.

Without them, I suspect that after the landmine explosion I'd have been tempted to grab the next flight home to Boston.

Upon her arrival, it was clear that my own mother needed some peer support, her own shoulder to cry on. Thank God for Ofrah, the matriarch of a family living in Moshav Avigdor, who adopted me during my stay in Israel. She was able to have a mother-to-mother heart-to-heart chat with Mom. It started with a hug. Ofrah counseled wisely in broken, accented English: "You cry . . . here in my house . . . here on farm . . . but with Jerry, you don't cry. . . . you strong for him." Ofrah knew something about this ritual. She had watched and cried alone for many frightening years as her four sons served in the Israel Defense Forces. My mother still feels a debt of gratitude to Ofrah. "She related to me as a mother. She was a real gift that came to me during the darkest time."

I needed the support of all my adopted friends and family in Israel. But call me high-maintenance; I also needed members of my immediate family to buy tickets to fly across the Atlantic to see, and understand, what I was going through. Otherwise the event would always remain this freak accident that happened to Jerry "over there" in the Middle East. My siblings came, as well as my parents, in serial tag-team fashion, to spend time with me while I was in the hospital.

After a month at my side, my mother flew home from Tel Aviv to Boston. And my sister Susan and my father came to Israel shortly thereafter. Susan wrote later about that visit,

> I felt deeply moved by the awareness of the horrifying pain and experience you must have been through but not reactive to the difference in how you looked. I have always adored you and knowing you were alive was such a relief. And also what had happened to you was so dramatic. It

changed everything and nothing at the same time. You were still you.

My time with all these people made me realize I was still a whole person, despite the loss of my leg. I was still me. It took me years to comprehend the extent to which my family and friends shored me up during these difficult months. For most survivors I have interviewed over the years—from New York to Jerusalem, from Sarajevo to Hanoi—the family plays a central and pivotal role in survival. Whether a spouse, a mother, or a child, I hear it repeatedly in survivor testimonies: *I would never have made it through without my family. They saved me during the darkest moments. I am closer to my family now, after my accident, than before.*

Sometimes it turns out that no one in the family is a great communicator—and some even inhibit emotional expression. That poses another challenge. Sometimes our families, seeking to protect us in crisis, discourage us from reaching out to find *new* sources of support. They may intend to protect us from the same big bad world that inflicted harm in the first place. Ironically, the same families who keep their wounded members from connecting with outside help also tend to prohibit expression of emotion *within* the family. On the opposite side, studies also suggest that a healthy family system can inoculate its members against the negative effects of trauma. Recent studies on familes who have a child with a chronic condition or disability found that a child's behavioral problems are not determined by the disabling condition.[1] When parents are both mentally and physically healthy and provide a functioning family environment, these factors will significantly enhance the resilience of a child in the first eighteen months after a diagnosis.

And sometimes family is simply not enough. We need our peers. After Jeannie's father died when she was thirteen she stayed home from school for a week after the memorial service.

> I felt like a different girl than I had been the week before and longed to be that predeath girl again. I dreaded going back to school.
>
> It was as bad as I thought. Everyone stared. People parted in the halls. I heard whispering. It's almost cliché. I didn't bother to grieve my dad. I just had to figure out how to get through my days without throwing up from anxiety or bursting into tears from loneliness. I wanted to be all fine, with a normal, intact family (not just living alone with my mom). I wanted to have normal adolescent friendships and hang out and listen to Fleetwood Mac. I felt envious and would cry when I went to houses full of siblings and happy parents and close relationships.
>
> Toward the end of eighth grade I met a girl who was new at the school and being shunned in that horrible, cliquey way thirteen-year-old girls do. I asked her over, and learned she was visiting from Germany while her father lectured at Stanford. We discovered we both were at the same level in piano and played endless hours of duets. We spent the summer swimming and touring. At the end of the summer they went back, and Tamara and I started a spirited correspondence.
>
> I started high school and decided to completely ignore the cliques and backstabbing and just do my thing—school, piano, art, church, work. Strangely, my social life took off. I had that idealistic "I'll just love everyone in my path" mindset, and it made me happy. I hung out with the artsy people.

I hung out with the nerds. I hung out with the stoners. I hung out with the jocks. And I went after God.

Jeannie survived by reaching out left and right and above, enlarging her family after her father's death. She in effect adopted a German family and started to build an international network of friends.

The challenge, of course, is that when it comes to families, none is perfect. But more often than not they provide a much-needed resource of social support. Think of it. Who are the first people you are likely to call in an emergency? Who can you rely on to help you move your home? Your brother. Your sister. Your cousin and nephew.

A feeling of support is needed in each dire circumstance. In fact, studies indicate that sometimes it is enough to perceive the presence of support, whether or not it is really there. The closer we are to our red-hot victim moment, the harder it is to look outside ourselves and understand the interplay of relationships. It takes time to comprehend exactly how much support from family, friends, and strangers is needed to overcome a crisis.

Christopher Reeve describes his time in the hospital:

I tried to focus on all the love and support that was coming to me. But much of the time I thought to myself: I don't care if anybody likes me or doesn't like me. I want to walk. I'll trade all this affection just to walk up a flight of stairs. The body and mind, in trying to survive, can be totally self-ish. You say, screw the rest of the world, take care of me. Me first. This is not fair to me, you know. . . . I think these self-ish thoughts are part of the survival mechanism. That "me-me-me" is an inevitable first response. And then you need to evolve to higher thoughts—a different way of thinking.[2]

I see reaching out as a form of "social oxygen"—necessary to sustain life. Without the ability to breathe in the reality of others around us, we can suffocate in our victimhood. Eventually, Reeve's accident motivated him to come to terms with himself as part of a larger community—one of more than 650 million people with disabilities around the world. Though he was not unique as a quadriplegic, Reeve's celebrity made him special and helped him advance the cause of spinal cord injury research and disability awareness.

Life and spirituality are nurtured in community, not in isolation. We are interdependent beings. In the end, no one survives or thrives on their own. We need family, friends, doctors, and fellow survivors to get us through tough times.

But what about the toughest, most hellish times? Even in the most desperate circumstances, we will find strength by reaching out to others. In the case of Edgar and Hanka, Holocaust survivors now living in Massachusetts, music was the key to staying alive and connected for over three years in a Nazi concentration camp in Theresienstadt, Czechoslovakia.

Having grown up in a country that focused heavily on cultural interests, music and operas were always a regular part of our lives. It stood to reason, then, that when rushed into camps with very few personal belongings, some people smuggled their musical instruments into the camp against the rules.

One of the heroes in our story was a fellow prisoner named Rafael Schachter. He was a pianist and chorus conductor, but because of the role he played in this camp, I refer to him as a "psychologist without a diploma." Rafael encouraged all men to gather in the evening in the cellar, to sing Czech patriotic songs. He managed to get the women's barracks to do the same. This brought our minds back to home and gave us strength to go on.

Edgar and Hanka tell me they would not have survived deprivation and imprisonment without the discovery of fellow musicians and a common cause. They also found an inspired leader in Rafael, who had the ingenuity and courage to keep people connected.

Sometimes it feels as if we have no instruments, we have no leader, we have nothing. That's when many of us call out to God. For many it takes a crisis, but in our darkest moments, most of us will reach out spiritually. It's a cry for divine help. We need someone—anyone—out there to understand. Our prayers reflect an existential plea for empathy in the universe. I believe this is a great and useful thing. I can't encourage people enough to pray, and then pray some more. Call out. Reach out. Your questions and search for meaning are enormously important. They reflect a desire to Choose Life and Reach Out simultaneously.

Whatever you believe, religion can offer a positive source of social and spiritual oxygen. Sigmund Freud argued that the interaction of social support and faith is inherent in religion, and that religion in fact exists because it reduces the threat to individuals of feeling lonely or rejected. Any reaching out— whether socially or spiritually—helps.

A study found that elderly open heart surgery patients who expressed faith in God had a survival rate three times higher than those who reported no religious faith.[3] Likewise, those who had the strongest participation in social groups also had a threefold survival advantage. This research suggests that a combination of religious faith *and* social participation in the community could provide a sort of protection in crisis.

So try it. Reach out and connect.

Ask yourself, who is your community in your hour of need? These are the people who will help save your life, and enrich it. Social support can come from unexpected quarters. Just getting out of the house and staying open to those around you—at church, school, bridge club, gym or neighborhood—will positively affect your physical and mental health.

One of my Vietnamese colleagues, Hoc, lost his hand, an eye, and a leg, and remembers after his accident feeling very self conscious, thinking no one would want to see him in his newly blown-up body. But he missed the social contact and finally got up his courage one day to go sit with his neighbors by the village well. "I didn't feel like talking for a long time, but I would sit and listen just to feel like I still belonged. One day someone asked me about cleaning up the well water, I started to tell them my thoughts. They listened, and that meant a lot to me. After a while, I was just one more village member trying to fix the well."

Someone who listens can change our world. Successful survivors are those who link to peer groups, friends, and relatives in order to break the isolation and loneliness that inevitably accompany tragedy. It's up to each one of us to reach out and reclaim our place in the world after a jolt. Social support may be the most important factor to save us from a life of chronic victimhood and isolation.

I am always impressed by the strong bond among veterans, including well-known American prisoners of war in Vietnam such as John McCain. Their military code of conduct inculcates an attitude of mutual survival, with duty to country and to family. When I first met Senator McCain over lunch in the Senate dining room, I was immediately struck by his stubborn survivor spirit. McCain credits his five-plus years of perseverance in the face of torture to his sense of duty to and camaraderie with his fellow navy men and prisoners, and a sense of honor instilled in him by the military careers and character of his father and grandfather. He writes in his autobiography:

> I had been greatly strengthened by the company of good men [in prison], and my resolve was firmer than it had ever been. I was sustained by the knowledge that the others knew where I was and were concerned about me. I knew they were demanding my release. And, most important, I knew they would be proud of me when I returned if I successfully resisted this latest tribulation.[4]

McCain's father was made commander in chief of the Pacific region during his captivity, prompting an offer of early release from prison, which the younger McCain refused.

> I wanted to say yes. I badly wanted to go home. I was tired and sick, and despite my bad attitude, I was often afraid. But I couldn't keep from my own counsel the knowledge of how my release would affect my father and my fellow prisoners. I knew what the Vietnamese hoped to gain from my release.
>
> Although I did not know it at the time, my father would shortly assume command of the war effort as Commander in Chief, Pacific. The Vietnamese intended to hail his arrival with a propaganda spectacle as they released his son in a gesture of "goodwill." I was to be enticed into accepting special treatment in the hope that it would shame the new enemy commander . . . I knew that my release would add to the suffering of men who were already straining to keep faith with their country. I was injured, but I believed I could survive. I couldn't persuade myself to leave.[5]

Survivor personalities find some moral compass to guide them. McCain and his peers held fast to the Navy Code of Conduct as a source of strength, even when they knew their actions were futile. When I first visited the "Hanoi Hilton"— the nickname for one of the Vietnamese prisons where Mc-Cain was held captive—it was clear that escape would have been nearly impossible.

The Vietnamese worked hard to prevent their prisoners from communicating with each other, both to suppress their morale and to prevent any chance of an uprising or escape. John McCain attempted communication at every possible opportunity, and was frequently punished with more beatings, deprivation, and isolation. McCain describes isolation as the hardest punishment.

> Communicating was the indispensable key to resistance. Without that, it was hard to derive strength from others. Absent the counsel of fellow prisoners, I would begin to doubt my own judgment, whether I was resisting effectively and appropriately. If I was in communication only for a brief moment once a day, I would be okay. When I was deprived of any contact with my comrades, I was in serious trouble . . . my isolation was awful, worse than the beatings I had been sentenced to for communicating.[6]

I believe it is indispensable to communicate with other survivor types to shore up our own inner survivor. On a visit to Texas, I had the privilege of spending a few hours with business leader and former presidential candidate Ross Perot. He shared with me some of his views on survivorship as we toured his sprawling Dallas headquarters, resembling a veritable museum to patriotic and humanitarian service. Sitting with him in his office and talking over lunch, Mr. Perot relayed story after story of heroism and survivorship. It came in all shapes and sizes, from a single mom putting her kids through college to a team of marines on a rescue mission in Vietnam. But Perot still can't say enough about his admiration for the highly decorated navy pilot Vice Admiral James B. Stockdale, his chosen 1992 vice presidential running mate who died in 2005.

Admiral Stockdale was shot down over North Vietnam in 1965 and spent over seven years as a prisoner of war, four of them in solitary confinement. The highest-ranking naval officer in captivity, Stockdale later wrote, "We organized a clandestine society via our wall tap code—a society with our own laws, traditions, customs, even heroes."[7] This helped create a culture of defiance among his fellow captives, including John McCain. One day, Stockdale was ordered to clean up so that he could be filmed for a propaganda piece in which he would play a visiting American businessman. McCain recalls how Stockdale was given a razor to shave:

> Jim used it to hack off his hair, severely cutting his scalp in the process and spoiling his appearance, in the hope that this would render him unsuitable for his enemies' purpose. But the Rabbit [his guard and interpreter] was not so easily dissuaded. He left to find a hat to place on Jim's bleeding head. In the intervening moments, Jim picked up a wooden stool and repeatedly bashed his face with it. Disfigured, Jim succeeded in frustrating the Rabbit's plans for him that evening.[8]

Admiral Stockdale was awarded the Congressional Medal of Honor in 1976, but where exactly did his resilient fighting spirit come from? No doubt part of it came from within. But it was also fueled from the outside—Stockdale was a patriot who understood how others were depending on him; his fellow officers looked to him for leadership. To survive, POWs like Stockdale and McCain must discover *social* purpose. They must learn to reach out in every way possible to connect with each other.

I believe it is very important to have mentors and role models, like Stockdale, McCain, Perot, and others, even if we've never met them. We rely on the example of leaders to motivate us—we *want* to be strong and to stay positive for *them*, even when we may be filled with self-doubt.

Staying positive is impossible for those who isolate themselves, particularly when you add depression to the mix. In studies on teenagers, it has become clear how isolated and apart kids feel. We are all nervous about letting people in to see our pain. The shame of it all. Possibly there is just too much stigma associated with what ails us. In can-do America, "self-made" men and women are not supposed to be needy or depressed.

Katya recounts the worst year of her life—junior year in high school. She had been dealing with severe depression since the seventh grade, but really hit bottom in eleventh.

> I'd get dressed in the morning, but the depression caused such severe anxiety that I wouldn't go anywhere that had a lot of people. Not even school. I lost all my friends in tenth grade, because I hadn't been that sociable. I felt lonely, hollow, scared, trapped, and hopeless. Depression warps your thinking, so when family and doctors told me to choose life, reach out, and get moving, I dismissed them. I thought, "Those things aren't for me—the rest of the world can do those things, but they're impossible for me."

Finally, the doctors prescribed medicine. I still felt like I was just a shell going through the motions but not really living. That's when I accepted that I needed help, so I asked to be hospitalized so I could focus on beginning my recovery. I was only hospitalized for a few days, but I used every resource offered—journaling, reflection time, individual and group therapy.

The depression had caused me to feel different from my peers. I never mentioned why I had missed school. I had one teacher, my eleventh-grade AP English teacher, Ginny Mitchell, who always had so much compassion, empathy, and patience with all her students. Her English class was a safe haven for me. She knew what I was going through and used her compassion, empathy, and patience to help me, but we never discussed the depression—we focused on English, my favorite and best subject. We dissected Faulkner's *The Sound and the Fury,* analyzed poems, studied for the AP exam among many other things. Ginny's classroom was a place where I could be a normal high school junior, and I needed normalcy. I wasn't sick in her classroom, I was just a seventeen-year-old doing my best work.

Light can come in the form of a single teacher, a mentor, an aunt, a big brother. Katya found hers in a high school English teacher. We thank God for the angels who appear just in time.

Adnan in Jordan says that making connections comes naturally in the Middle East. Networking is a survival skill. Adnan, a paralympic athlete who lost both his legs in a trucking accident, has more friends than anyone can count. He reminds me that social networking is as old as the descendants of Abraham, and as durable as the ancient stones of Jerash and Petra.

"Around here," he explains, "we have always understood the importance of connections and of helping others. This is how we've survived for centuries in Jordan, particularly with little water and no oil. It's the reason for our legendary Bedouin hospitality! Just imagine the growing network now being created by my eleven children alone!" Adnan leads by example, reaching out left and right to build social support for Jordanians with disabilities. And he insists his children do the same, building diverse connections whether through school, the local mosque, a community gym, or the marketplace.

Sometimes our social awakening is very slow. I think of a young woman we work with in Yemen. Raja lost a leg as a child and rarely left her house. She had been kept shut away by her protective Muslim family for years, always veiled, never looking anyone in the eye. Then we invited her to meet other survivors, always accompanied by one of her brothers or her father. And the miracle began. We brought her to a survivor leadership training in Geneva. She watched closely the role models around her—how they spoke, how they studied, how they laughed. She listened to a new vocabulary of empowerment and disability rights. Slowly, she emerged. She started to stare directly into people's eyes. Now, two years later, she is emerging as a leading advocate for the rights of women with disabilities in Yemen.

Sometimes all it takes is one meeting, or a new relationship, or a simple invitation to get out of the house to meet others "like you." People may resist at first, but then the miracle can happen. The "veil" is dropped, and a stronger individual emerges ready to live again. If we have a supportive social environment that satisfies our basic psychological needs (autonomy, competence, relatedness), then we are likely to grow stronger through adversity. But if our social environment is unsupportive and inflicts further stress (alienation, humiliation, and isolation), then we are more likely to develop unwelcome symptoms and pathology.

My own experience has taught me how crucial it was to be recovering with other young guys my age. We could joke about the things that interested us, from sex to sports to wheelchair races. Members of cancer peer support groups have been shown to achieve more optimal emotional functioning, and they indicate improved quality of life, better coping strategies for their illness, and enhanced attitudes toward their treatment.[9]

Research shows that *perceived* social support is more important in predicting positive outcomes than the actual support received.[10] In one study, the speed with which active-duty military men recovered from combat stress reactions was correlated with higher confidence in the availability of social support.[11] Simply knowing a resource is available can help someone through tough times. I can testify to the power of simply making peer support available in other countries. I have witnessed positive change in hundreds of survivors I have had the privilege to work with around the world. Change is possible even with survivors who previously seemed locked in depression and isolation.

It is also possible for those locked in lifestyle habits. Larry is a family friend who was like an uncle to my wife and her four brothers. He was quite the workaholic into his sixties, when he suffered a heart attack while driving one morning. Paramedics were called immediately, and shock paddles jump-started his heart. During his recovery, Larry reassessed his priorities—deciding to spend more time with his wife, his eight children, and his numerous grandchildren. Sounds like a cliché wake-up call, perhaps, but Larry stepped up his game. He took his wife to dinner and to concerts, spent weekends at the beach house with family and friends, and totally reordered his life. When Larry died suddenly at home only six months later, his family was so grateful for those final golden months with him.

Being open to others, willing to reach out, is key to a healthy life of survivorship. People can surprise us if we are willing and open to their support and counsel. Social support can come in all shapes and sizes: peer role models, siblings, parents, friends, a helpful neighbor, a teacher, kind strangers, or professional counselors as needed. There can be no more sitting alone in your room. Isolation fuels victimhood and decreases your chances for survival.

As social creatures, we all need to reach out, even when we don't feel like it. With the right social support, we can begin the process of planning our next steps to Get Moving. Keeping an active mind and body mobilized for health and work will transform suffering and ensure a brighter future.

6

STEP 4:

GET MOVING

♦

They say, "When the going gets tough, the tough get going." I always thought, "*Get going where?*" It's a fine motto for sports, I suppose, but it doesn't offer much comfort to someone who has been made vulnerable by tragedy or illness. Climbing out of crisis can require Herculean effort, physically and emotionally. We need to be tough to counter inertia and passivity. We must make our move against victimhood. But how can we leave our inner victim behind in the dust? Only by summoning energy and then stepping into the future will we find the next best stage of our life. There *is* life after loss. But we are required to act. It's about movement, and nothing gets done without it.

But it's no easy thing, particularly when our energy has been depleted by illness or misfortune.

Bobana's family used to enjoy paragliding as a family in Bosnia-Herzegovina. When she was twenty-three, she was supposed to go up with her dad, but she changed her mind at the last minute, so her mom took her place. Bobana looked up, knowing how much her parents loved to glide through the air. But that day, as Bobana watched, her mother and father were killed in a flying accident. Bobana was overwhelmed by grief and feelings of guilt. She tried to cope but couldn't shake her depression. So she plotted her own suicide, found a grenade, and decided the time had come. While working up the courage to slam the grenade against her body, it exploded. Both her hands were blown off, but she didn't die.

During her recovery, she wondered when she could try suicide again. One of my Bosnian colleagues heard about her and went to visit. Zeljko, an amputee himself, told Bobana that losing her hands didn't mean she couldn't achieve her dreams. Bobana was skeptical of that, but Zeljko challenged her to make a plan for her future. What did she dream of doing? "Forget your hands for a moment. What would you like to do?" Bobana wanted to be a photographer. Zeljko helped her research options, and she enrolled in a photography class. Friends helped her buy some photo equipment. She's now off antidepressants and pursuing her life's dream to become a professional photographer.

Bobana is on her way because she stopped living in the past and looked to what was possible in her future. She unlocked her inner survivor and *moved* toward a goal. Like Bobana, we need to devise our own personal action plan to set in motion the future we would like to have, even if it seems far off. *How do I really want to live the rest of my life? What steps can I take today?*

For me, it was critical that I not let others make decisions for me. I had lost enough power on the minefield and then lying on my back in the hospital bed. I needed to reclaim it somehow. Picking the hospital in Israel where I wanted to do my rehabilitation was one step in the right direction.

I've learned from working with war-injured people how important it is to develop very concrete plans to address the basic, practical problems facing each survivor in need. *Thanks for the fake leg,* in other words, *but it doesn't put food on the table for my kids.* Each person we work with in our Survivors Network must devise his or her own "Individual Recovery Action Plan" with specific objectives. They must be SMART: *S*pecific, *M*easurable, *A*chievable, *R*elevant, and *T*ime-bound.

This level of self-directed commitment helps build resilience. "I will start a class in carpentry in September." "I will get out of the house today and ask Lois to shop with me for groceries." "I will take the #9 bus to the prosthetic center this Thursday to repair my loose ankle." "To get some exercise, I will join the indoor volleyball team." You get the picture. Get moving, specifically, *toward* something.

Experts at the American Psychology Association concur: action and movement are essential for resilience. You must:

- take care of yourself
- move toward your goals
- take decisive actions

Almost any ritual can help a survivor reclaim a modicum of order and predictability. Becky turned swimming into a meditation, and not because she enjoyed it:

On April 2, 1987, I got a phone call at six in the morning: "Your mother passed away." From that moment on, I saw life in a different way. Besides all the normal emotional stuff—the grief of losing the most important person in my life, worries about my father and how he would cope, guilt about our less than perfect mother–daughter relationship—I got depressed. The kind of depression that means nothing brings pleasure, nothing seems worth effort. I wanted to drop out of life. I was afraid that I would stay like that—empty, hollow—for the rest of my life. Before my mom died, I used to swim laps four or five times a week. After the funeral, and when I knew my depression was more than normal grief, I knew I needed to do something to save myself, so I started swimming again. I made swimming the only obligatory activity of my life. Everything else—eating, studying, speaking—was optional. I almost never "felt like" dragging myself across campus, changing into a bathing suit, taking a shower, picking a lane, diving in . . . But I did it. I gritted through it. Some days I hated it. To say it was a battle sounds cliché, but it was a real battle: Becky against Becky. It was my way of fighting against my own brain chemistry and depression.

Becky's battle reminds me of the words of the artist Vincent Van Gogh: "If you hear a voice within you say 'you cannot paint,' then by all means paint and that voice will be silenced."

When I left the hospital in Israel it was like leaving a cocoon. They try to train you to face the outside world again: first it's a night out at the movies with volunteers, then the occasional weekend away. But finally, it comes time to fly home.

My new life began at the end of October 1984. After a long flight, I slowly made my way off the ramp at Boston's Logan International Airport. I was walking with crutches, a bit nervously. As I turned the corner, I saw my mother. She hadn't seen me for almost five months, and this time I was upright and walking. She was crying tears of joy. I don't think I realized how nervous my family was to see me. There was the first hug, eyes welling up, everyone united—Mom and Dad, siblings and friends. It felt like a lifetime had passed. But I was home at last. There were memories from Israel that would take me years to unpack. But for now, what a great relief it was to be back in small-town New England.

Looking back, I can see myself trading one cocoon for another. First, there was the rehab center in Israel, which had become familiar and safe. Then I went to the cocoon of my small hometown. When you hurt, you seek out comfort. And mine came in the form of familiarity. I could have stayed home forever, all that attention, with my family and friends waiting on me hand and foot. But somehow I knew that was not good for me.

I had to get back to my life, and out of my comfort zone. The time had come. I went back to college. Everything looked the same on campus, but people saw *me* differently. Why were some old friends avoiding me? Was I supposed to approach them first? What are the rules here?

I wanted my friends to feel relaxed, and to ask me any question they wanted, just not to be nervous around me. After all, I was the same person as before (except I weighed less). It was eye-opening to see how my new outward appearance, particularly when I was hopping on one leg or using crutches, affected the way people treated me. It was another revelation and lesson on how *not* to be when someone has gone through a trauma. But I remembered the AA prayer for serenity—to accept the things I cannot change, find the courage to change the things I can, and the wisdom to know the difference. Well, I couldn't change anyone's reaction to me, or their behavior, but I could work on my own. That's when I, like Becky, started swimming laps. It was something I could do that got me out of my dorm, out of my books, and out of my head—laps upon laps upon laps.

I can't emphasize enough the need for movement. Sometimes even the perception of making progress is important. "Laps" make my point. You are literally going around in circles, back and forth, and yes, the repetition is monotonous. But there is progress, too; you DO move forward, just by doing something. That semester I spent in the pool got me in better shape than ever, and more than that, it helped me get moving in the rest of my life.

We can get so desperate to change our circumstances that we will try anything. Dave, a friend from business school who is a soccer-playing stud, lawyer, and father in Virginia, was thirty years old and had reached his limit during his battle with mouth cancer.

> I was three weeks into an eight-week cycle of radiation treatment, and my mouth was covered with blisters. The skin on my gums was shedding like a snake's. I had to remember to spit the desiccated skin out so that I did not choke on it. But these issues did not lead me to the top of my staircase dressed for battle. It was the hiccups. Hiccups, of course, are normally dealt with by drinking a glass of water or holding your breath or eating peanut butter. Yet I had battled with them for over nine hours, and nothing was working. So I was going to try another old standard . . . SCARE them out.
>
> These were body-wrenching, chest-heaving, and spasmodic hiccups—the kind that make passersby cringe. My fiancée and I had already exhausted every remedy we knew. Scaring them out of me had to work.
>
> I still shake my head and experience a deep cycle of emotions when I remember catching a glimpse of myself in the mirror near the top of the stairs. I was emaciated,

exhausted, a fresh scar running from ear to ear across my throat. I had been through hell, and still had a way to go. Yet, there I stood at the top of my stairs blasting out hiccups like an old town news crier, wearing a bicycle helmet, soccer shin guards, and a puffy ski jacket for protection from injury during my plunge down the stairs, trying to figure out a way to fight my newest bogeyman.

Whatever's threatening you is big. And to beat something big, you need a plan. Once you have a plan, you have hope. I stayed firmly in the moment during that period of my life, and tried to knock down each challenge one by one. Now, five years later, I am fairly certain I had no intention of actually flinging myself down the stairs that morning to scare away my hiccups. But at the time, I had run out of all other options. Hatching this plan at least yielded the slightest bit of hope that I needed to survive until the sun came up and I heard back from my doctor. Turns out, these hiccups were a common reaction to some of the pain medicine I was taking. And there was a remedy.

"Once you have a plan, you have hope." Well said, Dave! In the worst physical or emotional suffering, even a semblance of a plan can help.

One of my favorite survivor guides on the planet is Helen. She is ninety-four and has never spared me her advice . . . because I ask for it all the time. I call her "Your Majesty" in deference to her royal wisdom. Recently I asked her, "What's the worst thing that's ever happened to you?"

The biggest challenge in my life, by far, has been losing my vision. I didn't need glasses until I was in my sixties. And now I can't see. I went to an ophthalmologist about twelve years ago, and he told me I had macular degeneration. Yes, I was forewarned, and it was gradual, but I absolutely hate it. I used to look at people's faces and see dark spots. This Christmas was the first time I couldn't make out if someone was sitting at the other side of the table.

Helen misses her vision terribly, but she doesn't draw attention to it. She tries to keep focused on others—sponsoring interfaith forums, advocating for peace, and following current events. I asked how she dealt with her loss of sight. After all, here is an incredibly bright woman—always ahead of her time—now facing blurring dark shadows in her nineties. "Aging isn't for sissies," Helen warns. So I ask her, "What do you do each day to keep going?"

I get really angry sometimes. But I try not to let it get me down too much. Someone once told me that if you are a worrier, then worry like hell for an hour. Then let it go. The same goes for anger, I think. Get really mad about something that's eating at you. I may take about twenty minutes to walk around the house in a snit, and slam things and just ignore the mess in the kitchen, refusing to clean up or do anything else but be mad. That helps. I never ask, "Why me?" I could just as easily ask, "Why not me?"

I do talk a lot to myself, and I write myself notes from time to time. "Dear Helen, you really have to get over this . . ." Then I tear the letter into pieces and throw it away. Even though I can't see, I still try to write things down. But mostly positive things, not any negative words. At my age, it's just something to do. I write words like 'Peace' and 'Sunshine' and 'Be Kind' and 'Thanksgiving' and such. I'm sure it looks like a mess on a page, because I can't even tell if I'm writing the words on top of each other, or whether it's legible. No one sees me do it, but I find that writing letters to myself is much better than keeping a journal, something I could never do.

Helen's daughter Mig is also a close family friend. Mig was in a life-threatening car accident at age sixteen that sliced up her face and left permanent neurological damage. "When I got out of the hospital," Mig said, "my face was like hamburger meat. I only learned later how my father had removed all the mirrors from the hotel suite, so I wouldn't be shocked by the damage." Mig was back in school even before plastic surgery was complete. Being with friends and classmates mattered most of all. Resuming a normal routine was Mig's way of moving forward. "What was I going to do? Sulk in front of a mirror all day long, pining for my old face?" Her family culture was more "move on and suck it up." Her mother recalls:

> It was November 1955. There I was a mother being so careful with each child and BANG—something terrible happens. When she got back to school, very fast, Mig was saucy about it. She would tell people who asked about her face, "I was eating peas with my knife!"
>
> I try to never dwell on anything. I just take it in and move on. That's what you did back then. You felt bad about it, all the time, but you kept moving on . . .

There is something comforting about action and movement. After the fact, many of us will confess to some odd behavior just after hearing horrible news. We need to do something—*anything*—to distract ourselves. Some people get busy cleaning, as if wiping counters and doing dishes will put things back together. I distinctly remember after hearing the news of my father's heart attack that I pulled out a calculator, determined to complete my tax return, even as I went online to make plane reservations to retrieve my father's body for the funeral. I rationalized that my father had insisted that each of his children keep their financial house in order. It was April 14, after all.

I now see my tax behavior as a transparent attempt to reassert control over my circumstances. When something awful happens, we are totally out of control. The world as we knew it is gone, and this is deeply unsettling. The survivor instinct is to get busy asserting control over *anything* that might submit.

There is, however, a danger when we get moving too fast in our grief. It's another form of avoidance, but still, I think it's better than paralysis. To outsiders, busyness can look like early recovery, but it is not. It's more like a cover—a distraction from the real thing. Unhealthy movement is when you stay busy rather than facing the facts of your feelings. We sometimes need to go back to square one and revisit the facts of what happened.

My mother recalls how she got moving a bit too quickly after the death of her father. She didn't face her dormant emotions for thirty-two years. While adamantly moving forward, she left pieces of herself in the past.

The week before I graduated from Catholic grade school in Winnetka, Illinois, my father died. He had been sick from pneumonia for only a week, and I was just thirteen. I never saw my father in the hospital, so I never had a chance to say goodbye. I was stunned, as were my two older brothers. Within weeks, I was urged by my mother to "get over it" when I cried. The usual emotional supports for a loss such as this were not common at that time (1940s). I coped by "going on" in my life, acting like a teenager and enjoying the high school and suburban life that came with the town.

What I developed during this time was an ability to cope. I did not feel, I just did. I acted out in small ways, and there was one teacher who observed me and connected my behavior to the death of my father. She told me it was time to stop doing that ("acting out").

Later, having babies gave me a wonderful "purpose" for my life. Busyness is a very handy coping tool. I was about forty-five, married and the mother of six children who were in their teens, when I reached an emotional dead end. I began to get counseling, and the first issue that emerged with the counselor was the grief at the death of my father (32 years before). I began to cry. It was this talking and crying and the help of Al-Anon's twelve-step program that awakened my emotional life. I believe that is when I began to deal with the traumas of my youth.

As we move onward and endeavor to stay busy after a crisis, we need to be mindful, checking periodically to make sure our "doing things" doesn't become a long-term substitute for "feeling things."

Elizabeth, the godmother of my son Jay, describes how her world was sent reeling after a phone call informing her that her husband's plane had crashed. Search parties were out, they had not yet found his body, but they didn't imagine there would be any survivors. Struggling to keep her balance emotionally, she returned to the stove, where she was making dinner for her eight-year-old son and five-year-old twin daughters.

My whole world slowed to the effort of putting one foot in front of the other. I realized I had my work cut out for me when one of my children told me she thought her life was ruined, at age five. I determined I was going to fight for them to know joy and all the pleasures of a happy childhood to the best of my ability.

I imagined myself as a tightrope walker carrying my three children on my head on a wire high above the earth. Our survival was tied to my ability to bear the weight and to continue to carefully move forward, to continue living. All the routines of everyday life were actually very comforting— clothes needed to be washed, meals cooked, schoolwork done. Being a mother helped. By the way, that same child said one day, ten years later, that she loved her life.

Chores. Exercise. Getting through the day. All of it re- quires movement. It takes hard work to heal properly. It's physical, mental, social, and emotional. No one can move for you. You must tend your own recovery, your bandages, your rehabilitation, your children. It's *your* responsibility.

Passivity achieves nothing. Work matters.

You won't sell a lot of Hallmark cards with *that* slogan. But it rings true for survivors. Dragana in Bosnia-Herzegovina describes how being able to work advanced her recovery from cervical cancer.

After my diagnosis I felt so fortunate to work with and for thousands of refugee families who have lost so much, some- times everything, and still find strength to go on, rebuild, create, laugh. I felt so connected with them. I felt honored to learn and draw strength from the enormous energy of others to whom unfortunate things happen.

It was very important for me to make sure my life did not stop. I continued working and started enjoying every day and every person I came into contact with in a deeper, more appreciative way. I spent the six weeks between the cancer diagnosis and my surgery being extremely active. I had a purpose and a plan that I was in charge of. It sounds funny, but it was my own individual strategic action plan with carefully defined activities and time frame, for two important sectors of my life—my health and my work.

For many, work is simply a means to the end of making money. But for many trauma survivors, work and its surrounding social network are critical to moving forward.

Researchers have examined the effects of unemployment, underemployment, or job insecurity on well-being. The picture is clear that increased unemployment and job insecurity are associated with lowered psychological well-being.[1] Work can be especially helpful to survivors of traumatic circumstances. It can function as a source of identity, self-esteem,[2] standing or prestige in the community,[3] role fulfillment in one's family, involvement in collective activities,[4] and meaning or purpose for life. Work, the experts agree, is essential to full psychological functioning and well-being.

One study connects improved emotional well-being with a return to work after a heart attack.[5] Despite equivalent mental health in two subject populations, those subjects who returned to work reported decreased emotional distress. This was true even when the subjects who returned to work reported dissatisfaction with their jobs! Apparently, grudging work is much better than no work at all.

Returning to work takes effort. *Staying* at work takes even more. So take each day as it comes and find stopping points along the way to rest up for the next summit. Marking our progress, even little steps, is a good discipline. It might be habit-forming, even if it is not exciting. Phil is an accomplished doctor and tenured university professor who had to get moving for years. Eventually, it paid off.

> I struggled with depression since I was nineteen. I couldn't stay in college, so I dropped out. I ended up in the Army during Vietnam. When you are depressed like I was, you feel like you are under water, or like moving in glue. I really had no energy to socialize. I went through a divorce. I left work for four months. Depression affected everything.
>
> I was lucky to find a great therapist. I would give 50 percent credit for my personal recovery to the therapist and my medication. But I had to do it, get myself to appointments and take my meds . . . I had to establish some semblance of a routine. I had to make myself take lunch breaks and visit a nearby church. I had to keep the wheels turning.
>
> I now see people homeless on the street, pushing their carts, moving along. I really admire their strength, even with all their problems, depression, addiction, whatever they are. They must be so strong to move through each day. I don't underestimate what that takes.

One of the most common reactions to crisis is feeling out of control. A sense of powerlessness in one's life is associated with increased anxiety. When we get moving, we enact control over our lives. And this is associated with a lowering of anxiety, depression, alcoholism and physiological symptoms.[6] It doesn't matter whether we *feel* like exercising our survivorship, we must get out of the house and achieve some goals, however limited, to reassert our power, particularly when so much in life is out of our control. Even our own bodies betray us.

Beth was delighted to be pregnant again. But it didn't last. One second she had high hopes, painting the room and preparing the crib; the next second she was struggling with her worst fears.

> The baby had no functioning organs. It stopped growing and couldn't produce the amniotic fluid it needed. After we faced the facts that there was no possibility that the baby could be born, and that my health and ability to have other children would have been compromised by continuing the pregnancy, we decided to "choose life" by having an abortion . . . It was an incredibly difficult period for me and my husband. But we got moving again mostly because we had two kids who needed us, and I didn't think it was so great for them to see their mom in bed crying. So I got up and played games with them and drove them to school and soccer and got back into life. If I hadn't had those kids, I'm sure I would have taken my time getting going again, so they were a really needed kick in the pants.

Beth was able to face facts, choose life, reach out, get moving, and ultimately give back to her community. She volunteered at her kids' schools, her synagogue and a local homeless shelter. Whenever she felt stuck, she says, she had friends and family to "pull her out of the stuck place." The good of her children demanded that she always be in motion, mentally, emotionally, and physically. Each and every cycle of survivorship requires movement and energy. Still, Beth cautions, "I think it's hugely important that people have some time to grieve and deal with their emotions *before* others encourage them to get moving. Most people can't do that immediately."

Debra agrees. Her husband, Herb, died at the age of forty-seven in his sleep of a heart attack. Like Beth, she got moving for the sake of her teenage daughter. She also credits physical exercise as one of the keys to her mental health. "I would walk along the Potomac River. Something about the water gave me a moment's peace. Or I would walk on my treadmill with music blasting." Volunteering came later, she says. "Helping those who may be less fortunate always helps make me feel blessed for what I do have."

Timing is key. Premature effort can exhaust someone with fresh wounds, sending them right back to bed, more discouraged than ever. You know the feeling, even after a routine bout with the flu. You get up in the morning, no fever, feeling ready to return to work. But by the time you're showered and dressed, your energy has evaporated. And gravity pulls you down, back under the sheets.

One key to success is setting achievable goals, even tiny ones. Whether we lurch forward or fall backward, we do well to remember the words of supersurvivor and statesman Winston Churchill: "Success is not final; failure is not fatal; it is the courage to continue that counts."

And sometimes, whether we like it or not, this courage comes in the form of a pill. For Martha to get moving out of depression and into life again, she needs to take her medication rain or shine. It is a daily discipline for her not to self-destruct.

Around 1990 a new class of antidepressant drugs came to market . . . like Prozac. My therapist suggested that drugs might be helpful and recommended a few psychopharmacologists to consult. One diagnosed my depression and liberally prescribed Prozac. All of a sudden, I was walking down the street humming a favorite song. But then the drugs triggered a manic episode that almost did me in. The fall from mania is deeply painful. I lost a lot of weight, but I also burned through $200,000 I didn't have . . . all in a twelve-month period.

After my doctor prescribed a drug cocktail to address both the depression and the manic sides of the disease, I started "living well through chemicals." I now take nine drugs a day and am closely monitored. When I sink into a black pit or start to race, he changes the cocktail. Our goal is to keep me even. And little by little, I've grown to like even. I have had to surrender to the fact that I need medication for biochemical stability.

There have been times in the past thirteen years when I did not want to take the drugs anymore. I sometimes feel controlled by these little bottles. But by sticking to my daily regimen, I experience the benefits of a more even emotional life.

To get moving requires daily discipline. For some, this means taking medication. We may not always like it, but we may need it to survive and stay in the game. It can help us get outside ourselves. For others, daily discipline can mean setting the alarm, waking up, getting out of bed, stretching, eating oatmeal, playing loud music while unloading the dishwasher. I have heard from some parents after the death of a child that it is enough to "put one foot in front of the other" to get out the door and face the world again. It can be excruciating, but any routine, however prosaic, can help.

No matter how hard we pray, no matter how many people we call, we still must exert physical and emotional effort in order to heal. You may have heard the story of Hercules and the Waggoner. A Waggoner was once driving a heavy load along a very muddy way. At last he came to a part of the road where the wheels sank halfway into the mire. The more the horses pulled, the deeper the wheels sank. So the Waggoner threw down his whip and knelt down and prayed to Hercules the Strong: "O Hercules, help me in this my hour of distress." But Hercules appeared to him and said: "Tut, man, don't sprawl there. Get up and put your shoulder to the wheel." The gods help those who help themselves.

George is one of those active, athletic guys who works hard and loves the outdoors. He wrestled in high school, got good enough grades to get into Cornell, and later joined the army. He was an enthusiastic hiker who was used to "feeling in control and secure." But pain in his degenerative hip chipped away at his spirit, getting worse each year.

> I spent four years limping in pain. I could only walk about one block. I slept poorly, trying to find a comfortable position at night. I remember feeling vulnerable having to use crutches and sometimes a wheelchair. I didn't like that feeling, as if I couldn't escape in an emergency.
>
> I couldn't go to the gym as much, and even then only working on upper-body strength. One day I was in a sports store. I saw a kayak. It was a chance thing. I asked about it and sat in it in the store. It hurt at first, but I took a risk. I bought it.
>
> I found I liked kayaking as much or more than any activity I have ever done, even better than hiking. I can kayak every day. It is beautiful and peaceful. It's great exercise and has even helped me with meditation and mindfulness training. Kayaking has brought me physical and spiritual release.

Like others, George got moving physically as well as mentally. The use of exercise and sports to contribute to psychological well-being is well documented. It is clear that there is an association between exercise and both short- and long-term well-being. Physical activity has been shown to be associated with higher self-esteem, decreased levels of mild to moderate depression (and is a good adjunct to the treatment of severe depression), reductions in neuroticism and state anxiety, and reduction in stress levels. These beneficial emotional effects have been shown across both ages and genders.[7]

I suppose it helps if you are already a champion cyclist. Lance Armstrong was diagnosed with testicular cancer in September 1996, and quickly learned it had already spread to his abdomen, invaded his lungs, and even reached his brain. His initial reaction was disbelief. He asked his doctor if he should get a second opinion. "How can you be so sure?" he asked his doctor. The response was chilling: "I'm so sure that I've scheduled you for surgery at seven A.M. tomorrow."[8]

Lance realized that his cycling had helped prepare him to face the trials of cancer.

> What makes a great endurance athlete is the ability to absorb potential embarrassment, and to suffer without complaint. I was discovering that if it was a matter of gritting my teeth, not caring how it looked, and outlasting everybody else, I won. It didn't seem to matter what the sport was—in a straight-ahead, long-distance race, I could beat anybody. If it was a suffer-fest, I was good at it.[9]
>
> The physical pain of cancer didn't bother me so much, because I was used to it. In fact, if I didn't suffer, I'd feel cheated. The more I thought about it, the more cancer began to seem like a race to me. Only the destination had

changed. They shared grueling physical aspects, as well as a dependence on time, and progress reports every interval, with checkpoints and a slavish reliance on numbers and blood tests. The only difference was that I had to focus better and harder than I ever did on the bike. With this illness, I couldn't afford impatience or a lapse in concentration; I had to think about living, just making it through, every single moment. The idea was oddly restorative: winning my life back would be the biggest victory.[10]

There it is again, that competitive survivor spirit. *I won't let this thing defeat me!*

To win, you need a plan of action. You need to exercise your options. There's a time for staying still, but eventually all survivorship demands movement. The speed at which you move is less relevant than the belief that you will move. I'm more a walker than a cyclist, so I draw inspiration from the words of our most melancholic and ambulating president, Abraham Lincoln, who used to say, "I am a slow walker, but I never walk backwards."

Walking forward means we must learn to give again. The survivors who convert their misfortune into blessing do so by giving back to their community.

7

STEP 5:

GIVE BACK

◆

How do we find the motivation to *give* after we have been sorely tested and tried, and all our resources depleted? Isn't it sufficient to survive our troubles? Isn't it enough that we've recovered? Frankly, no, that isn't enough. Because until we reach a point where we can be grateful for our life experience, we are at risk of backsliding into victimhood. We won't cross the finish line until we rediscover gratitude and learn to give again. Only then will we thrive.

It's an unfortunate fact that most of us take our blessings for granted. We get through the worst and want some credit for surviving. But unless we find gratitude, a way to give back, we do not complete the last cycle of survivorship. "A person starts to live when he can live outside himself," Albert Einstein said. And he was no dummy.

I often say I am the luckiest survivor in the world. I've had every opportunity for education and good health care. Every three or four years I get a new $17,000 prosthetic leg. I have an Ivy League education from Brown University and an MBA from the University of Michigan. I have a stunningly smart and beautiful wife, four healthy kids, and a cozy roof over our heads. The list of blessings has only grown in the years since my minefield experience. No one is luckier than I. I put it behind me and moved on. I had an international think-tank job, family, friends, and home, and was very comfortable.

Then I took my first trip to Cambodia. Cambodia has one of the largest ratios of landmines to population in the world. Anywhere you go in this vivid country, you will find evidence of decades of war.

I mentioned at the start of this book how I was resting one day by the side of the road in Phnom Penh. There was that little girl, who looked no more than nine, begging across the street. She had one leg and a wooden crutch. It was a very hot day. I was wearing shorts and had removed my artificial leg to adjust my stump sock. The young Cambodian rushed over to me, hobbling across the dusty road. She looked amazed at my robotic leg and then smiled big and blurted out in Khmer, "You are one of us!"

To this day, I feel ashamed of my initial reaction. I thought to myself, *No, I'm not. You are a poor beggar girl in Cambodia. And I am a big white guy from the States.* But I looked at her again, and suddenly I did see myself. We were alike. Right there on the roadside, something changed in me. It's as if my Grinch-like heart grew a couple sizes that day. I knew I could keep this new insight to myself. I could take my fancy prosthesis and college education back to the United States, with its fine medical care and laws designed to protect my rights. I mean, what could I really do to join this girl in the enormity of her daily struggle for survival? I would have turned away, perhaps, but for the echo of her voice inside my head: *"You are one of us."*

Yes, I am a person who is missing a limb. A random accident in a minefield in Israel injured me. But for years, I resisted the notion of being defined by my injury. Now I began to realize that I was part of a world of people who are too often denied their basic rights and freedoms. Because, as it turns out, in many countries, once you are "damaged" by war, you've lost not only your limbs or sight, but also your place in the community, your job, your family. My fate had seen me born in Massachusetts and not Mozambique, and that was the only reason I didn't also face these same struggles.

I suddenly felt I could not turn my back on this young Cambodian girl. I felt a tug on my life, and I knew I had to do something. It was time for me to give back.

I went back to Washington, D.C., and launched Landmine Survivors Network with my friend Ken Rutherford. He had been with me on that trip. We knew we were among the luckiest of survivors, born in America with freedom, opportunity, and means. But because of those opportunities, we could perhaps help others not so fortunate, including survivors in Cambodia, like that beautiful girl in Phnom Penh. We would try to help those people who had the same devastating injuries we had, but next to no resources or community support. We wanted to help all survivors overcome victimhood as a state of mind. And if we could do something about getting the tens of millions of mines up out of the ground, we would do that, too.

Our vision was big—a world where all people could fulfill their potential and contribute to their communities, living in peace. Survivors around the world would be united to help one another and to help eradicate this man-made epidemic. We had our work cut out for us. At the start of our International Campaign to Ban Landmines (co-recipient of the 1997 Nobel

Prize for Peace), nearly 26,000 innocent people were being killed or injured by landmines each year. Every twenty-two minutes there was a new casualty, and 80 percent of the victims were civilians, including thousands of women and children each year. In Cambodia alone, there were hundreds of new accidents monthly, and the Campaign estimated that roughly 1 in 230 Cambodians was already an amputee due to landmines. No wonder I saw so many limbless beggars on the street corners of Phnom Penh. It was surreal.

Our work since then has proved that with the right support, *all* survivors can heal and thrive. We've made over 93,000 home and hospital visits since 1997. We also know from experience that peer mentoring—survivors helping survivors— offers hope and motivation to work for a better future. You might say that the founding of our survivor network was driven more by a principle than a weapon or explosive event. That principle is the simple but profound determination to live, to thrive, despite the horrors of war. It's a personal decision to rise above "it," to refuse to let "it" stop us. Our choice is not to let our fate lie in the hands of the establishment, or culture, or other people's charity, but to seize our personal destiny and, once we've done so, help others like us seize theirs.

I also learned that by giving back to others, particularly after going through difficult times, you strengthen yourself. Why? Because you realize you actually have something to give. Making a contribution builds you up, too. When you are in a position to thank people who have helped you along the path, when you are in a position to give to strangers something of yourself, that means you are coming out of the forest of troubles. In our survivor networks, we hire and train more experienced long-range survivors to visit newer victims. These wily veteran visitors rediscover their own strength, and they see how far they've come. They also learn how they can serve as an inspirational and motivating force to accompany others out of the dark moments of isolation.

The key is to get out of yourself and into others. The extent to which your energy can go to more than mere survival is the extent to which you can learn to thrive in your lifetime.

There is a difference between surviving and thriving. Thriving requires tapping into our gratitude and drawing on this well to give to others. Studies on gratitude and giving are starting to proliferate. Why? Because people are catching on to the secret of happiness—giving, not getting. It turns out that by giving, we end up getting as well. It's a loop. Ralph Waldo Emerson said, "It is one of the most beautiful compensations of life that no man can sincerely try to help another without helping himself."

The gift of gratitude is ancient wisdom. Aesop, the Greek master of fables, said, "Gratitude is the sign of noble souls." Marcus Tullius Cicero (106–43 BCE), the Roman statesman and orator, said, "Gratitude is not only the greatest of virtues, but the parent of all the others."

But what if you don't have a lot? Can you still give? Of course. Families living in poverty are among the biggest givers relative to their means. Just travel through low-income villages around the world. You could be sitting in a one-room house without plumbing or electricity, but you will be fed like a king and served with abundant kindness. You may not deserve or appreciate it fully, but the fatted calf was sacrificed for you, a stranger in their midst. It's worth remembering that statistically the poorest are among the most generous. *Well, that's why they are still poor and I'm not,* you jest, *they should learn to save.* But seriously, does your savings account bring you joy? Does your bank balance make others smile? Have you ever given until it hurts, and then been surprised by how good it feels?

Generosity, it turns out, is an indicator of gratitude and happiness. Neuroscientists at the National Institutes of Health have scanned the brains of volunteers, asking them to think about a scenario involving either donating a sum of money to charity or keeping it for themselves. When volunteers placed the interests of others before their own, their generosity activated a primitive part of the brain that usually lights up in response to food or sex. Altrusim, the experiment suggested, is basic to the brain, hardwired and pleasurable. Just think of it. It was Saint Francis of Assisi who admonished, "For it is in giving that we receive."[1]

Giving is simply good for us. It can be private, public, big, or small. Dr. Martin Luther King Jr., said, "Life's most urgent question is what are you doing for others? Everybody can be great . . . because anybody can serve. You don't have to have a college degree to serve. You don't have to make your subject and verb agree to serve. You only need a heart full of grace. A soul generated by love."

Dragana, my Bosnian friend who survived cervical cancer, says,

> I do not want to live only for myself. I want to share what I have learned and what I feel with others. Not only through talking about my experience and educating other young women that cervical cancer does not happen to someone else, but through inspiring and motivating people to discover their inner strength and passion for taking charge in their lives and making this world a better place.
>
> For me, life is about enriching and making better the lives of people who are less fortunate than I am. And I feel very, very fortunate. For me, a day spent without making a difference in the life of others, even by a kind word, a smile,

is a wasted day. And there is so much more that each of us can give.

Hands down, absolutely nothing I have done in my life has compared with the transforming experience of meeting thousands of survivors and trying to be of help. I discovered meaning and growth in starting Landmine Survivors Network. I came to believe that we can all reflect on our circumstances and make meaning out of tragedy. For ourselves, for the strength of our communities, it is something we must apply ourselves to do. It's an act of grace—allowing a crisis to give us purpose. Fritz, one of the two friends who carried me out of that minefield, reflected years later that:

> The experience in the minefield has had an impact on my life that has grown with the passage of time. In the days and weeks that followed the incident, I experienced a lot of guilt. Why Jerry and not me? It must have been my fault. In time, this feeling weakened. But it wasn't until the beginnings of your work with other landmine survivors, that new layer of understanding began to take shape. The explosion which tore off your foot was also the first step toward the work of your lifetime. I look back at that moment of peril, of blind stumbling and frayed nerves as a crucial event, as the birth of something which has already done so much good and will continue to do more good in the world. It is an honor to have been an agent in this. At a simpler level, the experience has also taught me that the adventure you seek is not the adventure you will find. One can do no better than you in responding to this adventure with grace and sureness of step.

Fritz's kind words motivate me. Together, we find meaning in our mutual trauma. How? First we survived. Then we got healthy. Then, years later, we found meaning in the birth of a global network of survivors helping survivors. Fritz was an agent in saving my life and, in turn, has encouraged me in this life-transforming outreach to help others who are picking up the pieces after their lives explode.

In my work with war survivors, we do all we can to get them to give up their "victimhood." We *invite* them to move forward. We promise to *accompany* them in this difficult journey, *encourage* them to let go of past injury. But we can't force them to let go. Sometimes, there's not enough time in the world to hang out with victims who want to stay victims. Nothing you do or say can save them. It's their responsibility. That's the tough love of survivorship. There comes a point when you must move on, leaving victims to stagnate in their own choices.

What we try to get them to grasp is this: You must *give* to a community in order to *belong* to a community. You can become a volunteer, a community leader, a donor, a social change agent, a future peer supporter. You get outside yourself and, by doing so, get away from your suffering. It's not charity. It's not pity. It's gratitude in motion. It is belonging in action.

It's amazing how giving to others *triggers* gratitude. Sharing your story with someone else in need makes you appreciate how far you have come in coping with your loss. As Anne Morrow Lindbergh writes, "One can never pay in gratitude: one can only pay 'in kind' somewhere else in life."

I am endlessly inspired to learn of victims turning their lives around after loss, and then finding a way forward that blesses themselves and those around them. My friend Plamenko lost one of his legs to a mine explosion in 1992 during the Bosnian war. After the violence subsided, Plamenko set out to build a peer network of survivors helping others throughout southeast Europe. He introduced me to Ramiz on my last trip to Bosnia-Herzegovina.

Ramiz stepped on a landmine in 1994. He lost his right leg. He asked himself how he would feed his wife and a six-month-old son. His young family had no home. So Ramiz moved in with his parents, but he avoided his family, drinking heavily and falling into a deep depression.

Then Ramiz met Adnan, another amputee. Adnan told Ramiz he had to get back to his life, his responsibilities. Ramiz told Adnan he felt overwhelmed with the responsibility of taking care of his family again. But Adnan persisted, and Ramiz found support and guidance with other amputees. It took over a year, but finally this peer-to-peer support began to pay off. Ramiz joined a survivor economic support group and attended meetings for six months.

Armed with a business plan and new confidence, Ramiz built a greenhouse and a thriving tomato business. He became known in the community as honest and hard-working, and people lined up to buy his produce.

> I feel like I have eliminated that horrible feeling of uncertainty and insecurity. If it weren't for this opportunity, I would still be wasting my days drinking and my future would be uncertain. Thanks to the support from my community, my family has a strong husband and father again, and with my new business, our future is no longer uncertain.

But Ramiz went further than that. He wants to build a second greenhouse and hire other survivors. He also gives out produce to his neighbors in need.

The day I first donated 200 kilograms of fresh tomatoes to the local orphanage was an incredible moment for me. After so many years, I could now help others in need. I was no longer the beneficiary, but the benefactor.

After years of being in need, it is a thrill and a relief to become a giver again. That is the power of giving back. Ramiz has discovered the fifth step on a path to thrive, not just survive.

We benefit from belonging, from contributing to a bigger thing called community. We all have a role, with talents and gifts to deploy. Each act of generosity seeds goodwill. Even by listening to another person tell their tale of woe—thereby affirming their path—you can help build community. Each of us is born with talents and gifts. And they are meant to be deployed, not for simple survival, but for the good of the community. A body is also a metaphor for community, and if any one part is hurting, the whole body is weak. We need to shore each other up and make sure we acknowledge with appreciation people who pray, forgive, connect the unconnected, and serve the more vulnerable among us.

BT is someone who lifts up others. He is a survivor from Eritrea who was disabled in 1978 during the civil war.

At first I felt, "Now that my legs are injured, what is going to happen to me?" But I quickly dismissed these notions because I can't get rid of what happened to me, so I stopped thinking and worrying about what had happened to me, and I started thinking about going back to work. I started thinking about how I would lead my life. No one was going to do that for me. Slowly, all the bad thoughts started fading from my mind, until they were completely erased.

I now take care of my mother because she is seventy years old. In this area, there are several challenged people, and older individuals. If they can't cultivate the land themselves, I cultivate it for them, as much as I can. It means I hold responsibility for feeding those people. I work the land they can't work on, and I share the produce with them. And I also get to keep a share for myself . . . without them spending the labor. That is like help . . . it is not bad for them and I conclude that it's not that bad for me, either.

It's amazing how giving back can turn a perspective around. Most people in BT's community think *he* is one of the challenged ones, living with disabilities, but he certainly doesn't. Why? Because he is in a position to give.

One of my favorite in-laws, Julie, experienced her chemo treatments as a wake-up call to start living with purpose by paying attention to others. She thought, if only she could have a second chance—more time—she would try to be of service.

I knew it was bad when the physicians came to deliver the pathology report and couldn't look me in the eye. In that instant, my life had just changed forever. I had joined a club I wanted no part of.

Facing mortality is so personal and has a lasting effect, more than the ordeal of the illness and treatments . . . Looking back, I can't say what was the worst part of the physical assault to my body, but I know what was the most difficult emotionally. It was the realization that something could happen to me and I had not accomplished what I felt is most important in life. I had not been purposeful in my mind; I had not done anything that would leave a lasting mark or made any significant contribution. I remember thinking over and over, "God, don't reel me up yet, I'm not done." I hadn't really begun, and this fact kept me willing to cooperate and do my part through the treatments.

I am now a case reviewer for children in foster care, learning what I can in consideration of playing a larger role in the future, whatever that will be. It's the kind of thing I always wanted to do but never found the time. I have met so many children who have been dealt a bad hand already in their short lives. The knowledge of how fortunate I am to be in a position to try to do something on their behalf, and how many are in need of attention, keeps my mind on the future instead of the past.

Julie's mother and father had experienced tough things in life, and gotten past them. Her mother, Miriam, had lost her childhood home twice, survived spinal encephalitis, and had to learn to walk again after several weeks in a coma when Julie was just a toddler. Her father, Forrest, had contracted tuberculosis while in the service and subsequently spent over two years in hospitals, some while Julie was old enough to remember having to give him up to a hospital she was not allowed to visit. Julie and her two brothers were old enough to understand some of what took place in their young lifetime, but Miriam and Forrest shared their ideals of strength with their children. They demonstrated the value in helping others, the need to contribute and be purposeful, because there is always someone less fortunate than you. That was a part of their "giveback"—transferring stories of resilience from one generation to another and teaching the concept of taking care of others when and where you can.

Miriam shares how she survived life's storms. Her husband died only nine months before Hurricane Charley blew away their family home. Now seventy-nine years old, Miriam finds comfort and hope, giving back by volunteering to help others who are still dealing with the hardship, emotional and financial, that comes with losing your home and all your belongings.

Here I was sixty-seven years after we lost our home in the Merrimac River floods in the 1930s, with my idyllic world taken from me once again by the wrath of nature. At first I wanted to just give up. Without my husband beside me, I didn't think I could cope. But thinking back to my parents and what they faced in 1936 and again in 1938—the middle of the Depression, no insurance, and two young children to raise—I realized I wasn't really so badly off. I had insurance, and my three children and their families, though living far away, were there for me with love and support. One of my husband's favorite songs was "You'll Never Walk Alone," and I knew I was not walking alone. With their encouragement and help I "kept my chin up high and walked through the storm."

My world today is different from the one I loved and would have preferred, but it is one in which I belong at this stage of life, happy, comfortable, secure, and full of caring and supportive friends who also survived Hurricane Charley. We are a "family" of survivors who give each other understanding and encouragement and find that by helping others who are not so fortunate—and there are many—our volunteer projects give new meaning to our lives. Life goes on and so do we.

That's it, isn't it? Life goes on. But in our most vulnerable moments, we discover what we're made of. We can then align our unique mix of strengths and weaknesses to contribute to society. The family storytelling can be done in a way that is purposeful, beneficial, and contributes to personal healing. While we can't control all the bad things that happen, we can use our strengths to make a difference in the outcomes.

Vietnam veteran Claude AnShin Thomas suffered debilitation after he returned from war in Southeast Asia. He was prone to violent outbursts, panic attacks, insomnia, substance abuse, and a deep fear and hatred of the Vietnamese. He carried a gun every day for years after returning, and was unemployable and often homeless. His life was turned around when he began to seek help and was repeatedly pointed in the direction of a Buddhist monk and teacher, Thich Nhat Hanh, who has devoted his life to promoting peace and reconciliation between North and South Vietnam. Thich Nhat Hanh was exiled from Vietnam and nominated by Martin Luther King Jr. for a Nobel Peace Prize. Awakening spiritually and learning from other Buddhists helped Claude turn his life around.

> I [had] hit bottom, a place where the pain was so intense I didn't know how to hold it. I thought my only option was to die. As we wake up to suffering, we may feel at some points as if we might explode . . . The practice of mindfulness and meditation have provided me with invaluable resources and tools in those moments, in those hell places. They also help me to be able to go to those places with others, to support them in caring for and healing themselves.[2]

Claude AnShin became a Zen Buddhist monk, traveling the world to teach others about nonviolent thinking and lifestyle. He gives back by speaking and writing about how to overcome fear and stop feeding aggression, hatred, and violence. He specializes in counseling others who survive traumas in which the individual has had some complicity—a victim and victimizer rolled into one. Claude tells me that healing is available to everyone.

> This change of thinking is something anyone can do, but they have to want to live differently, and some people are so embedded in their worldview and so fearful of letting it go that they have become attached to their victim status, and this makes change impossible for them.
>
> For a long time I really didn't know how to change. I had to "wake up" from the fog of my intoxication and addiction. I remember my first sober date was May 28, 1983. I tried many times to clean up, but didn't have any knowledge about the disease of addiction, or the proper support, so I failed on my own. I kept falling back on managing my unmanageable life by self-medicating. I turned to prescriptions instead of illegal drugs. Whenever I developed a problem with a certain prescription drug and quit taking it, my doctors would go through their list until they found one I hadn't tried. I'd convince myself that this was okay. Rx's seemed more justifiable, but I realized that the substances would change but my patterns would not. I eventually let them go altogether.
>
> The first place I received peer support from others was at a treatment center in New Hampshire. This was a very powerful experience and absolutely critical to my recovery. People I have watched try to quit on their own almost never succeed in creating a new relationship with the world, so they fall back into old patterns.

Claude AnShin is a strong believer in peer role models, encouraging others to take their pain and turn it into action that will hopefully help prevent others from experiencing that same pain.

I think of many others who have found giving back meaningful, such as Carolyn Weghorne in Dallas, a mother whose son developed bacterial meningitis at boarding school outside Philadelphia. He was already unconscious when she arrived at the hospital. He was dead within twenty-four hours. Carolyn co-founded the National Meningitis Foundation with other mothers who had children who either died or were disabled by meningitis. The sole purpose of the foundation is to notify all parents whose kids go to school, college, or camp to get the meningitis vaccination.

Mothers Against Drunk Driving (MADD) was founded by Candy Lightner after her thirteen-year-old daughter Cari was killed by a drunk driver. Since MADD began in 1980, the number of annual drunk driving accidents in the U.S. has been cut in half.[3]

Alcoholics Anonymous was founded in the 1930s by Bill Wilson and Bob Smith, two alcoholics desperate to end the addiction that was destroying their lives. When medical approaches failed them, they sought a spiritual approach, and the kind of understanding and honesty they could only get from a fellow addict. The pillars of peer sponsorship and spiritual development are still at the core of the modern AA.

There is also the Compassionate Friends, started in 1969 by bereaved parents Bill and Joan Henderson and Iris and Joe Lawley after their sons, Billy Henderson and Kenneth Lawley, died just three days apart in the Coventry and Warwickshire Hospital. The Lawleys decided to send flowers to Billy's funeral, initiating a friendship in which the two couples met up regularly to talk through the memories of their boys and the pain of losing them. Soon, another grieving mother joined them, and they decided to organize as a support group and reach out to other parents who were grieving for lost children.

Lance Armstrong—now synonymous with "Live Strong"—incorporated his foundation to support cancer research and advocacy, giving cancer patients the tools and strength they need to survive. He started the foundation while he was still recovering from an aggressive treatment for the testicular cancer that spread through his body. He was grateful for the chance to regain control by helping others conquer cancer as well. "The foundation seemed like the perfect answer to the limbo I was in: I had completed chemo, and beaten back the cancer for the time being, but I had to figure out what to do next. To work on something outside myself was the best antidote."[4] Lance told me once that he thought landmine survivors and cancer survivors probably had a lot in common. The causes of trauma might be very different, but the long road to recovery is very familiar and similar.

The point being, whatever the affliction, the journey to find meaning—to make a positive contribution to others—is crucial to full survivorship. There are many things waiting to bring us down, pulling us out of giving. We're tired. We've been through enough. We have our work and our families. No one thing might keep us from giving back. More often it's a combination of circumstances and environment that congeal into inactivity. But it is gratitude that brings us up again. The thirteenth-century Christian mystic Meister Eckhart said, "If the only prayer you said in your whole life was *thank you* . . . that would suffice."

Surviving hardship can lead to gratitude, which can lead to giving. I think of Diana, Princess of Wales, as she turned her life around after separating from the Prince of Wales. She very deliberately and publicly threw off her victimhood and chose life. "There are so many people suffering who I think we can help. I just want to make a difference in peoples' lives, to be a force for good," she said as we traveled the back roads of Sarajevo.

In the time I knew her, Diana began to find her own voice, to understand that she had something unique to contribute to the world—her genuine gift of compassion. When she said she wanted to be the "Queen of People's Hearts," she meant it. Her gifts were real, remarkable, and deeply intuitive. During the last year of her life, Diana was winning her own battle to live with purpose and meaning.

Princess Diana told me how much she loved Mother Teresa, the Albanian-born Indian nun who founded Missionaries of Charity. She had met her on a couple of occasions and they recognized in each other, I believe, similar gifts of compassion and caring. In her thirties, emerging from the pain of her divorce, Diana was awakening to her own ministry of survivorship. Mother Teresa died unexpectedly on the eve of Diana's funeral. Like most survivors who learn to give back in life, Mother Teresa was a servant who worked tirelessly for others. Giving sacrificially was her mojo, even to the point of chastising those who didn't get it. It was Mother Teresa who said with characteristic tough love, "If you can't feed a hundred people, then feed just one."

I call my survivor comrade, Ken Rutherford, a supersurvivor on steroids. He is constantly crossing new thresholds of survivorship in an effort to better himself and give back to the world. And he does it with pace and confidence. In 1993, he was working as a training officer for the International Rescue Committee in Somalia, where his job was to help Somalis apply for microcredit loans so they could escape poverty and start rebuilding their country. On December 16, he was inspecting a program site near the border with Ethiopia when his car hit a landmine. The explosion thrust Ken into years of painful struggle, but I'm not sure I've ever seen someone cycle so quickly through all five steps of survivorship. This guy will settle for nothing less than thriving. But it comes, he says, from his capacity to face facts and choose life, and his determination to reach out and give back. And for Ken, giving with gratitude is the crown and glory of a survivor's journey. Listen how he cycles through the five steps:

1. **FACE FACTS.** *After the explosion, I first remember seeing a foot lying on the floorboard of the car. I remember thinking: "Is it mine?" It was. I kept trying to put it back on, but it kept falling off. Then I looked at my left foot. The top part was ripped off and I could see bones going to my toes, one of which was missing. Facing facts for me was death or life. I have dreams going back to that time—on my back critically injured in the Somali desert—thinking maybe the accident was all a mistake and that if I could put my foot back on before rescue help arrived they would never know and then the accident would never have happened. I now believe my near-death experience fundamentally affected my perspective on life—that every day is a great day. Without near death, I doubt I would have that attitude.*

2. **CHOOSE LIFE.** *I dragged myself out of the car and called for help on my radio. It seemed like a lifetime before help arrived. While I was waiting, I prayed to God. I was spitting up blood, so I thought that I might have internal injuries that could be fatal. I asked God that if I lived, I would like to marry Kim, my fiancée of two months, and raise a family. In the evacuation plane from Somalia to*

Nairobi, a Belgian doctor and an American nurse gave me blood, directly from their bodies to mine.

In a period of thirty-two months I had ten surgeries and countless procedures and rehab sessions to save the left foot. Finally, I had to make one of the hardest decisions in my life—and against the wishes of my doctors, who kept trying to "save" the remains of my left foot—to amputate. Up until then, I completely thought that I was going to beat this accident and live with one leg, which was doable. But not having any legs?

The decision was excruciating. But surprisingly, the hardest part was emotional and not physical. I had never thought I could have a good life without any legs. Waking up the morning of the amputation surgery, I was comfortable with my decision and pleased that I would soon be rid of my leg and the physical pain. I believed that in time I would again lead a full, active life and not be denied my dreams of being an active father, supportive husband, and professor.

3. **REACH OUT.** *I remember feeling alone one night. Really alone. Reflecting on what to do, I finally asked everyone to leave my hospital room, except for Kim. When the room cleared, I asked her to come by my bedside, and then I asked her to leave me. She didn't have to fulfill our engagement, as I was a different person now. She said to never say that again, and that we would get married soon. A few weeks later we set the wedding date and planned the ceremony with Kim at my bedside. Thankfully, Kim's physical and mental strength to convince me that we would be together and that everything would work out, and the Lord's presence, allowed me to constructively focus on what needed to be done. I no longer felt alone. After moving to D.C., I also I met another survivor—you, Jerry—and my Georgetown*

professors, colleagues, and friends, who have all added to my blessings with encouragement to stay active.

4. **GET MOVING.** *For the first few weeks after surgery, stump pain and phantom sensations controlled my life. Subsequent to being discharged from the hospital, the days were bittersweet. I was in love, and I was learning how to walk again. I had been told that there was a slight chance that I could walk for my September 10 wedding. My impending marriage to Kim had sustained my optimism. The most important dream was to marry Kim. On my wedding day, I felt like closing my eyes during the whole ceremony and reception to savor the moment. I felt like I was the luckiest guy in the world. It was a feeling of incredible joy that Kim would be my wife the rest of my life. It was the most memorable day of my life.*

I kept moving forward for my career and for what was best for family. Not looking back. Not thinking about disability but as a competitor. The end result is that after weeks of intense pain and nearly total mental and physical incapacitation, the pain left me. Now, besides infrequent stump blisters and infections, it is not as painful as when I walked on my mangled left foot on a daily basis. Postamputation I have an active lifestyle, including picking up golf!

5. **GIVE BACK.** *Seeds of bitterness cannot take place in a grateful heart. I am here today because of the resources I had at my disposal. I had a radio to call for help and airplanes to evacuate me. Most victims are not so lucky. I was given another chance to serve people. I do that by giving my time, serving on the board of directors for the Survivor Corps,*

working as teacher, a father of five, and supporting my wife in nursing school. I also serve on the Wilson's Creek National Battlefield board and the board of advisors of UC–Irvine Center for Unconventional Security Affairs.

After being so close to death, and then pursuing my teaching and parenting dream, I realize my life is more wonderful than I could ever have imagined. It is a force in perpetual motion. I feel my body and mind overflowing with gratitude and wonder where it will take me next. While I provide guidance, there are many times when my life propels itself. I feel as if I have the world in the palm of my hand more than ever. I can still achieve whatever I want to do with my life even though I don't have any legs. Today, I am overwhelmed by gratitude.

Today, Ken Rutherford is a tenured professor at Missouri State University, where he teaches political science, international relations, American citizenship, and democracy. He has testified before Congress and the United Nations and published a slew of articles in academic and policy journals. Strengthened by his catastrophe, he continues to advocate for a landmine-free world and rights for all.

To give back, we must sometimes go back to square one: Face Facts. We reflect on how far we have come from our moments of crisis. We list all the people who have helped us along the way. We see a strength and resourcefulness we never knew we had. We are grateful for life. And we show this by sharing it with others, particularly those who might be in the earliest stages of their survivorship. As the saying goes, "When you dig another out of their troubles, you find a place to bury your own."

To give back means to share. You can't keep yourself to yourself. There is more in us than we think. As a survivor, you are in a unique position to inspire others to heal and fulfill their potential. Thriving requires it.

8

ESCAPING THE VICTIM TRAP

◆

Why do some people stay victims? Well, it's strangely comfortable—a kind of defense mechanism after disaster strikes. We welcome sympathy in our hour of need. And then we invite it. Eventually, we must break the victim habit and resume taking full responsibility for our future.

After what you've read so far, you can see clearly that to thrive, you must work for it. Surviving is not a passive activity. But, similarly, it takes a certain amount of effort to stay a victim. So where will you put *your* energy?

Let's examine what feeds our inner victim. Perhaps the most notable characteristic is an attachment to the past, pining for the way things were before the Fall. *If only* . . . we could go back in time and make it right. *If only* . . . people could understand what I went through. *If only* . . . I had had a more supportive family or partner. Our victim voice can whisper or scream, even sing a sad country tune if necessary. We recognize alternatively the whining pitch, despairing sigh, or even an implied threat in this voice, even when delivered with a smile. Sometimes our inner victim surprises even us, when its voice escapes unedited from our mouth.

I said that? Really? Well, it's true, isn't it? I'll stand by it.

Our inner victim will do whatever it takes to be heard and heeded. It can play a seductive siren song in our head, drawing us in to sympathize and nourish it. And it feels good at first to be owed things, to feel wronged.

The Victim Voice can be highly manipulative. With practice, we victims become masters at eliciting feelings of sympathy and guilt in others, usually for not doing or caring enough. The aside: *"Oh, no one understands what it's like . . ."* The hint of blame: *"Well, you didn't just go through what I went through . . ."* The barb: *"Well, that's easy for you to say, you didn't just lose someone . . . "* It can also be as subtle as, *"I didn't get the e-mail; no one told me about the meeting today . . ."*

Victimhood is not just negativity or pessimism. Rather, when I speak of a victim-minded person, I am referring to an individual who is *stuck* in resentment of past and present circumstances. He or she can't seem to let go. These are individuals so focused on their own personal suffering that it interferes with their ability to take positive action, relate healthily to others, or participate more fully in daily life.

Victimhood, left untreated, will pull us down to the grave. It is not the same as depression, although clinically depressed people can show signs of full-blown victimhood. The primary symptoms of victimhood are blame and resentment. If only this and this hadn't happened to me . . . If only so and so hadn't done this thing to me . . . *If only* . . . Left to fester, victimhood fuels an obsession with self that leads to destructive behavior and narcissism.

Kathryn understands what's at stake if we don't take responsibility for our own lives and stop blaming others. She is an incest and abuse survivor. She now works with people living with HIV/AIDS in Africa. But she is intimately familiar with the lifestyle of victims and victimizers. She lived as a drug dealer until she was thirty.

> For fifteen years I drank and drugged all around the clock. I used to think I deserved to be an addict. I spent years blaming myself. I have been sober twenty-five years now. Since sobriety, I am on a journey to stay alive.
>
> I can tell when someone wants to stay a victim. But I really don't have energy for people who waste my time and don't want to work the program in AA. I went to three or four meetings a week for over twenty years. I became very particular about who I would choose to sponsor. I don't go there with whining victims . . . too much negativity.
>
> Victims want their holes filled by others. And I can't force someone to acknowledge their fear or inadequacy. Too many people don't want to take a hard look and learn from us who have already been there. There are just too many people who are in serious need and invisible — individuals who are being used and abused and left to die — but really want my help to find their voice and live.
>
> As a survivor, I can't keep quiet anymore. I just can't. I believe my job is to appreciate every moment I have been given. As a survivor, I have a purpose on this earth. And it is okay for me to speak up.

Victim personalities are relatively easy to spot, even when they try to hide. They often live isolated and alone. Victims prefer to keep their distance, unless of course their misery is lucky enough to find the company of sympathetic listeners. But what sort of life is carrying our baggage around with us, disconnected from community, feeling numb? There are those of us who have lost our survivor way because we are too busy indulging our inner victim. Sure, we may dress well and drive fancy cars. But if we are succumbing to victimhood, we are never going to be happy. We are denying our future potential, hurting ourselves and others in the process.

Victims can be found anywhere. They're the people whining about not being invited to this or that event. They're the ones bemoaning life's unfairness—unless it's doling out special favors for them. And even then, a victim will find cause for complaint. In their own controlled misery, these people can never be happy, for themselves or others. Why? Because a victim always measures, and *always* comes up with a deficit.

That said, some victims can be positively charming. I think of Eeyore, the lovable blue-gray donkey from A. A. Milne's *Winnie-the-Pooh* stories. He lives all alone in the House at Pooh Corner that is always falling down, which he calls his "Gloomy Place." Even though he is only eighteen inches tall, twenty-seven inches long, and stuffed with sawdust, Eeyore enjoys a huge following, including many adults, with numerous web pages and online discussion groups dedicated to him. His "Favorite Thing" is being remembered on his birthday. His biggest problem is that his tail keeps coming off. You can just hear the deep melancholic sigh as Eeyore serves up a sampler of victimlike sayings:

"Thanks for noticing me."
"If it is a good morning."
"It's all the same at the bottom of the river."
"It's not much of a tail. Most likely lose it again."
"After all, what are birthdays? Here today and gone tomorrow."

Like I said, charming. Cute, even . . . coming from a donkey. From a person, not so much.

Victimhood is a needy state. You can feel it suck energy from a room, whether in an office meeting or at a Paris bistro on a sunny day. You feel yourself pulled down by a victim's gravity force. Your eyes may feel strain. You steal a glance at your watch, wondering how much longer this person can moan. Finally out of sight, you let out a big sigh, as if to cleanse yourself and inhale new and more positive energy.

Helping a victim get out of the mind-set can be one of the hardest things in the world, because, first, a person must face the fact that he or she has sunk into a victim mentality. Maybe it began legitimately—this person was victimized—but it has evolved into a state of mind. How do we snap out of it?

In my work with survivors of war, for example, I've learned that outreach requires clarity of purpose and tough love. This means holding steady in the face of difficult emotions—to avoid the strong temptation to "rescue" someone who is suffering. We cannot "save" anyone but ourselves. We can offer support, but I try to be very clear about what I am willing to do and what I am not. It's enough of a challenge to save myself, keeping my own attitudes and life in order. I would just as soon avoid too much contact with whiners and complainers than give them what they need to move forward. I confess, it is much easier to hang out with friends who are already on the survivor path than those on the victim path.

If you give of yourself to a victim, you must do so carefully, with clear parameters. If you don't watch out, you'll be doing more harm than good. How so? It's similar to an addiction. When you are living with an alcoholic, you quickly learn how an addict can and will find any excuse in the world for their behavior. They must drink, therefore they deserve to. If you aren't vigilant, you are brought into the victim web of rationale and deception. A friend of mine who used to drink tells me, "Believe you me, no one can manipulate quite as well as an addict who needs to. I know from experience."

Victims *must* get what they need: at the end of the day, they are net takers. They draw in much more than they give out. And ingratitude is their dominant sin. After all, who has time to be thankful when we are nursing our own wounds? Beware: victimhood is insatiable—feed it and it will grow; reward it and it will spread like a virus.

Colleen is a survivor of childhood abuse, one of the worst cases I have heard, but she refused to stay a victim.

Childhood was about survival for me, my sister, and my brother. When Dad returned from Korea after some life-altering experiences, he was diagnosed paranoid schizophrenic. From the war he brought china for my mother, a new dress for me, a very warped mind, and drugs. Home was the only unsafe place I knew.

The torture he had endured at the hands of the North Koreans played out in countless ways at home. Dad saw things we didn't see. Puppies were enemies. He stomped them to death. Bugs became food—he cooked them—hundreds of them—in a big pot on the stove and tried to feed them to us. My nose was broken at four months and my feet were crisp with third-degree burns at six months. My first sexual invasion occurred before I could walk. My brother had both his shoulders dislocated at six months and was thrown down a flight of stairs at two. I became his protector and would have died to save him from any more harm. My father once took my younger brother to his work and held him by his feet over a pit of battery acid, describing all the things that would happen from burning in acid.

He set our house on fire and imprisoned us with his daily

and unpredictable insanity. The kitchen in our house was the scene of many bizarre family gatherings. Russian roulette at the breakfast table, and target practice for anything he could throw at my mother. It became a makeshift operating room where my dad felt he needed to cut the evil out of us. He once strapped my sister to an ironing board and collected knives, preparing to operate on her.

Who would blame Colleen if she decided to pack it up early, and spend the rest of her life raging at the torture she experienced at home? Yet now, in her fifties, she is one of the most successful and articulate "thrivers" I know. She says it took years of brutal honesty and therapy, but now Colleen is a successful senior manager at a large corporation. One of the ways she gives back is by applying herself to the human resource challenges of her company. If people are content and productive at work, she projects, then maybe they'll be happier and not abusive at home. Like the rest of us, Colleen much prefers working with those who want to better themselves, rather than chronic victims.

I can spot a victim from a distance and usually try to avoid them whenever possible. When forced to work with them, I sometimes get a sick feeling inside, similar to the queasiness you'd feel close to the edge of a cliff. I'm uncomfortable being near the kind of thing that could have swallowed me had something not been different in me, or for me. Honestly, I don't like that side of me. It feels a little unfair. I just know I have been given the power to survive, and I won't let anything or anyone dilute that power.

Whatever it is that gave me the courage and will to last, intact and hopeful, through the ordeal of insanity, is available to any and all of us. I simply grabbed for it when I needed it. First, though, I had to believe it was there.

Clearly, victims aren't always "those people" out there, or across the room. Look in the mirror. Sometimes it's you and me. It is very tempting to grow your inner victim, because it is normally rewarded. From an early age, most of us are taught that whining gets attention. "The squeaky wheel gets the grease." And even as we cringe at the high-pitched voice demanding attention—*now*—we think: *Please, just throw the child a cookie—maybe that'll quiet him down!* If, as a culture, we don't do something to stop nourishing victim behavior, we will end up with one of the most unresilient generations of all time, an exploding population of spoiled, victim-minded individuals, weakening societies around the globe. We will have to break some of these habits in ourselves, in our homes, and in our places of work if we want to move to a survivorship society rather than settle for a victimhood club.

Each of us can take steps away from victimhood and toward survivorship. It doesn't matter whether we are fighting big battles or small, we can change our minds about how we think about life's struggles. This is crucial, for how we think is how we become. Bill, a forty-three-year-old father in Seattle, reminds me of Helen Keller's dictum, "Although the world is full of suffering, it is also full of overcoming it."

It's never far from my mind, even more than a decade later. The day I sat in a soundproof room with my eighteen-month-old daughter on my lap—hearing small, and then increasingly louder sounds she clearly couldn't. It was the final step in the diagnosis of a rare birth defect. One that could, and likely would, lead to the complete loss of her hearing and eyesight.

My first child. The greatest joy of my thirty-two-year-old life. The one person in the world who I had a sacred obligation to protect and care for, and there was literally nothing I could do.

I went through a period of several weeks where I didn't sleep more than two or three fitful hours a night. I would do things like try to take a shower or go through my lunch hour with my eyes closed. Doing anything I could to get some sense of what blindness would mean. Then I'd go through the same routine with earphones on, to get a sense of deafness and blindness together. We enrolled in sign language classes, and spent hours doing research. It wasn't making me feel any better. It was sending me into a deep hole.

As a person who was most comfortable when in control, I had to devise some sort of plan that put me back in control again. That allowed me the chance to become the protective father again. The one person she could always depend on.

As long as I was alive she would never have to be afraid. Never have to go on a bus alone, or be vulnerable to traffic or dangerous people when walking down a street. I would be her eyes and ears. I would devote my life to learning what I had to do to be her bridge to the world. I would lie in bed and wonder what it would be like to spend the rest of my life devoted to my child. Convincing myself that it was the noblest path. Drifting off to sleep.

I specifically recall the time sanity returned with a thud. We were sitting in a doctor's office discussing options, and he noted that, at the end of the day, my wife and I were not raising a pair of eyes or ears, we were raising a beautiful, luscious little child. A child full of potential and possibility.

And it hit me. I did have a responsibility. My job was to

be a kid's dad. Nothing more, nothing less. To raise this kid so that no matter what she faced in this life she would face it with courage, and joy and determination.

Today, Sage is thirteen (going on eighteen). She's in a gifted program at her public middle school, and driving her parents crazy, because she thinks, like most teenagers do, that her mom and dad are a couple of idiots. Too much makeup, and too little clothing. Too much attitude, and too little interest in cleaning her room. Bliss.

Her eyes are worse. Her hearing is worse. But life goes on as it should. Every day her parents forfeit a little more control, and she gains a little more control. I can't wait to see who this little soul is going to become.

Bill had to make a deliberate decision to let go and equip his daughter to cope with her own condition. Certainly, he guards, he watches, but he knows the best gift he can give her is positive support and freedom to become.

So make a choice—choose to nourish the survivor in you and in others. Find your inner thriver and ignore your inner victim. Look at the five steps again and again. Starve that negative energy out of you if you must. And watch out for the five hallmarks of victimhood:

1. **LIVING IN THE PAST** (*Do you talk about it more than the present or future?*)

2. **SELF-PITY** (*Do you hear yourself whining a lot? Feeling sorry for yourself?*)

3. **RESENTMENT** (*When was the last time you celebrated another's good fortune?*)

4. **BLAMING** (*Do you point fingers and avoid taking respon-sibility for your behavior?*)

5. **TAKING** (*Do you act selfishly, expecting more than you are willing to give?*)

When we exhibit any of the above victim symptoms, we will distance ourselves from others, unintentionally alienating them. We can unwittingly suck energy from a conversation or a relationship if we don't watch it. But with some vigilance, you can reclaim a more positive attitude and posture.

You can climb out of the victim trap by literally tracking how you think and speak. You can write down the people or circumstances in your past that still have a hold on you. They can be negative, like a beating, or positive, like forever replaying your senior year in high school when you were prom king. How long have you been blaming or romanticizing the past? Look at your list and ask how important this stuff is to who you are and who you are trying to become. Next, write down everything you have to be grateful for. Be specific and don't rush this part. If taking inventory of your blessings feels like a chore, press on. For a breather, shut your eyes and think about things you absolutely love, from ice cream to sex, from beaches to barbecues. Recall your favorite Motown dance music, or songs that inspire or comfort you. Volunteer this week at work to help someone you don't know so well, or invite a new colleague to lunch or coffee. And the next time someone invites you somewhere, surprise them by reciprocating, buying tickets to a local comedy club. Meanwhile, turn off that new reality TV show and look up a new charity online. Yes, go ahead, give. You can spare $20, but stretch a little out of your comfort zone. Press the donate button, and then think about one of the smiling kids you just helped. If that doesn't activate that part of your brain triggered by generosity, then get moving out the door. Volunteer at a homeless shelter, a foster care program, or building homes for lower-income families. Get out of yourself. Get into others in your community. Throw a party, breakfast, lunch, or dinner, exercising your hospitality muscle.

I could go on. By now, you should understand that you must *do* something. Only you can decide what works best when you need to climb out of a funk. Be a survivor and take charge. When in doubt, on a cloudy day, just activate any one the Five Steps.

You won't undertake anything more important than this: Find your thriver within.

9

BUILDING RESILIENCE
TO TRAGEDY

◆

Now that we've dealt with defining victimhood, how can we learn to embrace resilience? Why are the survivor voices in this book so *damn resilient* anyway? What's their secret? Where do they find the capacity to rise above the ashes of catastrophe?

I'm here to tell you that survivors are everyday people in the car next to you, behind you in the grocery store, next door mowing the lawn. I meet these people everywhere, from every walk of life, on every continent. I only wish I could share more of their stories. I hope their examples will teach and inspire you to want to thrive. Just think: if someone can overcome that level of crisis or abuse, then maybe I can hang in there, too, just long enough to get through my crisis.

What is resilience, exactly? Resilience refers to our capacity to bounce back and resume function and health after a confrontation with disruptive or traumatic events. It's about elasticity and resourcefulness. Resilient people are somehow able to draw on past experiences and find inner strength to navigate their troubles and make the transition to a healthy, flourishing future.

The path to positive survivorship I have described in this book, with its action-oriented guidance, is drawn from the lived experience of survivors themselves, including my own. But there is real science and years of research behind it.

I think it's important to look at how trauma inflicts its damage. Humans have suffered from injuries, conflict, and natural disasters throughout history. But it wasn't until 1980 that we put a label on the residual effects of trauma: post-traumatic stress disorder, or PTSD. Since that time, PTSD has become a popular area of research, in part because it is considered one of the only psychiatric disorders whose cause is an external event. It wasn't until the mid-1990s that research about the consequences of mass violence and war broadened to include studies of social, cultural, moral, and spiritual factors that influence our human response to trauma.

Allow me to boil down some of the research jargon. Put simply, traumatic stress—not just everyday traffic jam stress—is caused by a confrontation with helplessness and death, a complete loss of control. And it is more common than you may think. Life seems to lose meaning and predictability. Our worldview is altered. From childhood, we all develop expectations about how the world will treat us. We are influenced by our upbringing, personality, cultural norms, and belief system. After a catastrophe, new information must be thought through until the negative experience is integrated into a new worldview. This is what we call the coping process.

Thankfully, most of us will never fight in a battle, witness a massacre, or find ourselves trapped in a minefield. And many of us will muddle through adversity without ever exhibiting any dramatic psychological scars from their trauma. Why the difference? It turns out that nearly every survivor of disasters, injuries, or assaults will face either positive or negative long-term consequences. What intrigues me is that positive outcomes—growing stronger through crisis—are not at all uncommon.

Am I suggesting that disasters bring blessing? Yes, depending on how we respond to them. In many cases, crisis will catalyze unexpectedly positive outcomes. But again, this happens only if we *decide* it will, if we are willing to search for meaning and purpose and thereby rediscover our common humanity. It's not the crisis itself that is important, but how we respond to it. Hundreds of survivors I have met describe how they grew stronger post-crisis.

There is a new term for it: post-traumatic growth (PTG). Also called "adversarial growth," I am referring to the development of positive attitudes and goals that can come out of even the most ghastly experiences.[1] Researchers now believe that PTSD and PTG actually result from the same mental processes. A survivor experiences predominantly negative or positive consequences depending on events and feelings they experience *after* the trauma. As we discussed earlier, strong and caring social support can ensure growth, whereas isolation and social antipathy will foster the symptoms of victimhood. So resilience isn't about the depth of trauma we experience, but, rather, about what we think about our trauma—how we process our personal nightmares.

Hurricane Katrina was an awful experience for hundreds of thousands of people. A study by Harvard Medical School evaluated the emotional responses to Hurricane Katrina from a cross-section of New Orleans residents. While almost all respondents reported feelings of intense stress, grief, and fear during and after the event, the study also found that the vast majority of people reported significant postcrisis growth:

- 88.5 percent reported an increased sense of meaning and purpose in their lives.
- 77.3 percent reported an increased feeling of spirituality or religious faith.
- 85.9 percent reported an increased awareness of and confidence in their own survival abilities and inner strengths.
- 89.3 percent felt they were now better equipped to cope with future stress.

Respondents specifically reported having discovered these strengths after, and as a direct result of, their experiences with the disaster. Surprisingly, higher incidents of post-traumatic growth were found in populations that were already marginalized and experienced a lower quality of life before the storm, such as minorities and the poor. They had fewer material and financial resources to fall back on, but developed even stronger emotional resources and felt more optimism and hope than their more privileged counterparts.[2]

Wow. Reread the paragraph above. The vast majority of survivors seem to have been jolted by crisis into increased purpose, stronger faith, higher self-esteem, and more resilience. They are feeling *enhanced*, not diminished, by catastrophe. There is something important happening, and it is not the result of Prozac or years of psychotherapy.

Leading theorists are working to develop something called the Post-Traumatic Growth Inventory (PTGI) to assess the extent to which an individual has grown stronger and more resilient after a traumatic event.[3] Post-traumatic growth involves a positive evolution in people's personalities and social life. For instance:

- *Interpersonal relationships* are improved; friends and family are valued more, with greater openness and self-disclosure and increased compassion and altruism.
- *Self-perception* is changed, and there is increased self-reliance. "If I have coped with this, I can cope with anything." Paradoxically, there can also be a sense of greater vulnerability.
- *Life philosophy* is altered, with survivors renegotiating what really matters to them, realizing life is finite, and reassessing their understanding of existence and spirituality.[4]

How do we make sure we fall into the PTG group and not the PTSD group?

My first tutors in the rapidly advancing world of neuroscience and resilience were Dr. Dennis Charney (a dean at Mount Sinai School of Medicine in New York) and Dr. Steve Southwick (a research professor at Yale University). Vietnam vets are a major source of their data, particularly those prisoners of war who never developed depression or stress disorders. Charney and Southwick tell me they were especially struck by the role faith, spirituality, and humor played in getting the most resilient soldiers through their toughest physical and psychological tests. Based on their research, here are the top ten characteristics of resilience: *Optimism; Altruism; Having a Moral Compass; Faith and Spirituality; Humor; Having a Role Model; Social Support; Facing Fear; Having a Mission;* and *Training.*

Complaining is obviously not on the top ten list. What strikes me about this research is that resilience seems to be something we can incubate and grow. It is in us and all around us. And, apparently, it's predominantly social. (Notice that there's no mention of self-reliance.) At least seven of the ten characteristics, in fact, we can choose to develop and *do*. I take great comfort knowing we can *learn* to become more resilient. It's not just a question of our DNA or upbringing.

The other encouraging news is that tough times can be good for us. Life experience will nourish and make us stronger. For example, studies of emergency personnel indicate that having survived one traumatic experience increases resilience and, in a sense, inoculates workers who will face subsequent traumas at work.[5] Most of us can point to early life experiences that afford us at least some practice in building resilience.

Although my small-town life was admittedly privileged and sheltered, I was exposed at an early age to life-and-death issues that may in fact have helped prepare me for my date with the minefield. There were the deaths of classmates in high school and the divorce of my parents. One winter night when I was about twelve, there appeared to be a growing ball of fire burning outside my window. Our next door neighbor's house was on fire. My mother ran through the house to wake and collect her children. It's the only time I remember her counting us out loud. One, two, three, four, five . . . where is the sixth? I heard panic in her voice as she screamed for my older sister Lisa, who was found brushing her teeth in her bathroom. Gathered around my parents' bed, we dropped to our knees in prayer for Mr. and Mrs. Vosoff. I closed my eyes tight and squeezed my hands, praying my hardest for this kind elderly couple who used to pass me candy and quarters for weeding their garden path. *Please, God,* I begged, *save them.* But no, they were trapped inside. I overheard one of the fireman saying how he found Mrs. Vosoff "crouching and charred" in a corner as he carried her out in a body bag.

It left an indelible impression. Another tragedy. Another prayer unanswered. Dare I say, another lesson? How strange that the tragedy of others—the deep sadness we brush up against us in our childhood—serves to teach us, somehow prepare us for living. Another terrible thing had happened—and I was still alive. Upon reflection, I suppose each visit to a hospital emergency room, a funeral parlor, an orphanage or nursing home, incrementally opened my eyes to the potential for danger and sadness, but also to endurance and the gift of life.

Josephine Hart observed, "Damaged people are dangerous. They know they can survive." Every time we come through tough times, we should feel some sense of pride and achievement. After all, getting through the experience may have been the hardest thing we've ever done. And we might be surprised to discover an inner voice and competitive spirit coaching us: *I refuse to be taken out by what happened to me. I will not be defeated by this. I still believe in the possibility of the future.* Even when our loss is the death of a beloved, and we may not feel like going on without them, we still honor their memory by healing and living strong.

From the first day I was injured, I wanted to go through it "well," to heal fully, whatever that took. Now, when storms of crisis come my way, I think back to what it took to heal mentally and physically from that minefield, and I am not easily derailed.

My friend Becky has a lovely daughter, Anna. Anna was born three months premature and lost her twin sister at birth. Becky doesn't bemoan what they both had to go through. Instead, she connects suffering with strength, both for herself and little Anna.

When I took my daughter Anna to see a pediatrician for the first time after three months of specialists in the neonatal intensive care unit, the doctor asked me if I had ever been through tough times before. I told her yes, that my mother had died, suddenly and unexpectedly, at the age of fifty-one, when I was twenty-eight. The pediatrician didn't say anything, but I knew what she was thinking. "This mom will be fine. She'll hold herself together. She just needs to know how to handle this baby, when to give which medicine, how to change oxygen tanks, and when to call me . . ." Looking back on this, I think my doctor knew that people who have survived one trauma will survive subsequent traumas. "Emotional toughness," I've heard it called. Trauma-proofed would be another name. I wonder now, nine years past those times, about people who spend their whole lives trying to achieve or maintain smooth, easy lives for themselves or their children. I wonder if life without tough times is less good for us. Maybe we actually need "bad times" to teach us how to cope with them. Maybe we need to experience hardship, disappointment, pain. Maybe we need to be forced to keep going despite our fears . . .

Now Anna is nine years old, and she has her own brand of emotional toughness. She holds her head high, literally, to show the scars on her neck, when she sees someone with a tracheotomy or on oxygen. She tells them with that posture and with her eyes that she knows what it means to have trouble breathing. I've seen it happen several times, in the Metro in D.C., or in a shopping mall, this glance of understanding that passes from her to a person who has a trach tube or an O_2 pack, and I see how strong and tough and compassionate she is. Because she had to fight for her life so early on, she is already tougher in some ways than many adults I know.

So, believe you can be strong. The Five Steps are doable. You will get through and become even more resilient. This is an important perspective, and implies a call to action. Come one, come all, gather around, and listen up. The time has come to stop running from our troubled childhoods. We don't have to like being abandoned or abused, watching our parents fight and divorce, but we can be stronger because of it. Experiences can be hateful. But we can appreciate how we have learned to toughen up emotionally. Let's stop complaining about everything that went wrong in the past—a habit of victim-speak—and start getting grateful. Think of it: your difficult upbringing and losses have made you more resilient than you may think.

I am encouraged by this focus on inner strength and health, rather than on sickness and symptoms. Some doctors and psychiatrists I have met seem a tad stuck in old-fashioned medical models of mental health and trauma recovery. Grief counseling, for example, as practiced by some psychologists in the United States and Europe, was not especially helpful to me and several of my friends. It somehow becomes more about surveys and acronyms than about rebuilding resilience and relationships. It turns out that naturally resilient individuals are not especially helped by grief counseling. Some people, like me, would prefer to share with close friends and family members. Others might want to share with peers, strangers, or a professional counselor. Letting someone choose their preferred means of support is critical. Good practice is about empowerment and choice. And with practice, survivors learn to go after what they need as they increase their emotional strength and build resilience for the future.

Resilience is there for the taking, for all of us. All we have to do is want it. Reach for it, and, as the verse promises, "Seek and ye shall find." Half the battle is believing we are up to the challenge: "I *will* get through this well. This will *not* take me down." Then get busy. It's not just the "other guy" who will inspire with his strength and grace—it's you.

10

HELPING OTHERS GET
THROUGH CATASTROPHE:

Or, How to Not Make Things Worse

♦

I work with families touched by war and terror around the world. You'd think it would get easier for me to handle horrible news. You'd think I'd become immune. If only it were true. Confronting another person's tragedy is one of the hardest things a person can endure. It's filled with all sorts of "shoulds"—things that are easier said than done. I confess that at times I have failed miserably to live up to my own standard, trying to demonstrate empathy in action. I never underestimate the discipline and strength required to accompany someone through their darkest hour.

When that landmine exploded on April 12, 1984, it wasn't just my personal date. It was a date for my mother, my siblings, and my friends. Each of us needed to learn in real time how best to give and receive comfort from one another.

So, how do we help someone other than ourselves when trouble comes? The phone rings in the middle of the night. We hear hesitation, a tearful voice, and you know the news is not good.

"Aunt Nancy was hit by a car last night . . ."

"I was just attacked in my apartment . . . can you come to the hospital?"

"Mom had a stroke and can't eat or speak . . ."

"The sonogram is showing something wrong with the baby's heart . . ."

"Cousin Hank is back in rehab . . ."

"The funeral service is Thursday, can you make it?"

Heart in mouth, we struggle for words. *"Oh my God, I can't believe it . . . Are you okay?"*

Each time I find myself in a family's living room while they are going through a painful experience, I must pray for grace and wisdom. It takes enormous restraint to be helpful, not harmful, in the midst of a personal disaster. But I have come to believe that this is the ultimate service. Each of us, at several points in our lives, will be called on to assist others during a crisis turning point, even unto death, knowing that what we do next will have far-reaching consequences—either positive or negative. We also know that helping others makes us grow.

Still, why is it so difficult to walk with others through the "valley of the shadow of death"? Probably because we have no map and things are out of our control. We don't want to do harm. But we must learn to become part of the supporting cast, even putting ourselves in the role of a servant. And unless you are a born Mother Teresa or professionally trained as a nurse, minister, or counselor, none of this comes naturally. It takes practice. And caregivers need support, just like survivors in crisis, as Tirza, a college student in Israel, attests:

I was nineteen when my father died suddenly. He was the dearest person in my life. After seven days of mourning, I went back to university. I remember sitting on the lawn in the sun, and another student waving and approaching, saying, hey, haven't seen you for a while. I replied so matter-of-factly, "I wasn't here for the week, my father died." Too matter-of-factly because inside I was screaming bereavement but acting too self-sufficient to reach out, let in, ask for comfort and acknowledgement of the pain.

Years later, I accompanied a close friend through her illness up to her death . . . The same temptation is there: to be the all-coping, all-functioning, self-sufficient person who gives support. Luckily—strange to use this word in this context—luckily, I break at one point. It is after forty-eight hours with no sleep. My friend is in the room almost unconscious with pain and refusing more help. We are on my friend's porch, going in circles. My friend's partner, the doctor, and myself no longer have a clue how to get through the next few days, how to cope with this last stage with death approaching. I find myself at a complete loss. That's all I feel, lack of sleep, crazed and pained, and I say, "I don't know about you guys, but I need help." And, thankfully, there was someone there for me. I contacted a friend from many years back—she specializes in spiritual accompaniment of people who are terminally ill. Speaking and consulting with her gave me a lot of strength. It was exactly the kind of support I needed, so I could make more peace with this tragedy and give better support to my friend.

When you are the one suffering, the pain is yours. And there are steps you can take to get through. On the other hand, watching someone you love go through intense pain can be even harder. You feel helpless as they writhe physically or emotionally. You must work very hard to keep emotions in check, try to understand what is really going on, and refrain from doing harm or adding to the pain.

The maddening thing is that you cannot rescue someone who's suffering. You are powerless to change the behavior or feelings of anyone but yourself. You can only assist and be present. My mother writes about watching me in a hospital bed in Israel:

> I have learned the only thing you can do for a situation like this is to "bear witness"—bear witness to the agony of your beloved child. It is a form of being there and keeping company. And not go to pieces and cry out your own outrage. When I sat in the hospital room with you and witnessed your excruciating wrenching phantom pains, I wanted to scream. I wanted to soothe . . . I wanted to suffer for you . . . There was no ointment, no bandage, no pill, no magic, and no prayer that could give back what you had lost. I couldn't make this one better. I felt numb, angry, and helpless, out of control, afraid, grieving, and deserted by God. But I kept trying to make it about listening to you . . .

My colleague Kristan still struggles with the year she watched her father die from a rare cancer in 2005.

> I am slowly getting over his death, a death that seemed premature to any one who knew him. I am, though, still sometimes having a hard time with the memory of his pain and suffering that last month. I have a hard time with what I witnessed, watching him suffer, physically and mentally for hours and days on end. It is very hard to see a loved one suffer, and it's harder when it's your dad, the person who has always been strong and fine and fit and there for you. But I

also recall the very special moments, tender or funny, we shared when he was in the hospital, and I'm grateful to have been there.

We are biologically wired to respond to the distress of our fellow human beings. A mother leaps up when her baby cries. Someone is upset, and we rub his shoulder to soothe. But before we run into the burning building, we need to consider donning some protective gear and bringing tools appropriate to work among the flames of victimization. You don't need an advanced degree. Anyone can learn skills to help others through catastrophe.

Your ability to listen is an essential gift of compassion to survivors. It can be draining, even vicariously traumatizing, to listen to someone describe in detail their personal horror. Just resist the temptation to give advice, and literally bite your tongue before offering the glib, "I understand." Allow the survivor to talk. Say, "I don't know what your loss is like, but if you want to tell me about it, I would like to listen." If a person doesn't want to talk, wait and ask again another day.

One technique, if we can call it that, is simply to "LUV" someone—Listen, Understand, and Validate.[1] This approach was developed by resilience specialists Dr. Lennis Echterling, Dr. J. Edson McKee, and Dr. Jack Presbury in the Psychology Department at James Madison University. Some of the suggestions below may sound frightfully scripted, but my hunch is that most of us need a refresher course in active listening, particularly if it's been a while since we've come face to face with overwhelming pain. I've taken the liberty of paraphrasing some of their guidance here.

Listen: What are some things you can do so a survivor feels listened to?

- *Watch your body language; face the person with an open and engaged posture.*
- *Maintain good eye contact, and lean toward the person with an expression of concern.*
- *Keep your composure and poise (i.e., don't gasp), even while listening to traumatic detail.*

Understand: How will a survivor know he or she has been heard and understood?

- *Repeat or paraphrase what the survivor is saying.*
- *Say what you think the survivor means and ask for a confirmation.*
- *Speak in a way that mirrors the survivor's mood and manner by using words and expressions that are similar to those used by the survivor.*

Validate: How do you convey your belief in a survivor's own strength and resilience?

- *Nod affirmatively and slowly as the person speaks.*
- *Smile with warmth and understanding (not broadly or with nervous laughter).*
- *Offer encouragers, interjecting rarely: "I see"; "Hmmm"; "Yes"; "Please, go on."*
- *Communicate your faith in the survivor's handling of the situation. You convey confidence by not dispensing glib advice or false assurances.*

When you give unsolicited advice, it sends an inadvertent message that you don't really trust the survivor to know or choose the best course of action. By offering instead a listening ear and supportive presence, you communicate respect for the survivor's own inner resources. And by bearing witness to the survivor story, you honor the individual's struggle to find meaning.

The second fundamental technique for crisis intervention is asking open-ended questions—ones that help survivors tap into images of inner strength. Our experts, Echterling, McKee, and Presbury, remind crisis interveners:

> Your role is neither the rescuer with all the power nor the expert with all the answers. By taking the attitude of "not rescuing" and "not knowing," you invite people in crisis to share their stories and to create their own positive resolutions . . . you are constantly looking for the survivor. In fact, by your manner and questions, you are inviting the person in crisis to join you in this search. To help you look for the survivor, you will be using questions, which can be powerful crisis intervention tools. Questions gather information, of course, but more important, they communicate important messages. By asking about strengths and coping, you invite a person in turmoil to pause, reflect, and dig for material that can be used to piece together a response that holds promise for resolving the crisis.[2]

When I first came across this approach to crisis intervention, I felt so relieved. Finally, I thought, some experts are advising on the basics of humanity and empathy. It wasn't your typical diagnostic approach, focusing on sickness and symptoms. Their approach draws on recent perspectives from positive psychology and emotional intelligence. It seems to me that very few people in the world of public health or humanitarianism have been trained this way. For many, it is so tempting to step in and probe for details about the crisis, because we are naturally curious about all the circumstances. But probing for *too* much detail can be counterproductive because it focuses on the victimization rather than resilience. If you have ever been interrogated by the police after a car accident or burglary, you know the drill: *"Just the facts, please!"* But when you are in the business of promoting resilience, it is far better to ask more open-ended questions that explore strengths, resources, and possibilities. Such questions will encourage the survivor to call to mind images of surviving and thriving, rather than past details of victimization. It is crucial to encourage friends and family members to search for the survivor by acknowledging the "crisis talk" while persisting in "survivor talk."[3]

Try asking a survivor such things as, "When you have had to face any trauma or danger in the past, how did you manage to handle it?" This type of question presumes inner strength and past experience. Or you could try something like, "How have you been able to cope up to now?" Again, this is a way to focus on what's working, instead of what is broken. Our goal is to help crisis victims see themselves as survivors: inherently strong. The fact that a person is alive is already evidence of his or her ability to survive. Some questions along these lines might include: "How did you manage to handle things the way you did?" "What did you draw from inside yourself to make it through?" Ultimately, what we want to do is fuel the inner survivor rather than feed the inner victim.

Okay, by now you are recoiling from the idea of a script. And you should. Authenticity and genuine caring can't be scripted. But knowing how to communicate with few words is a disciplined skill that can be learned, body language and all.

Navigating times of crisis with grace is like traveling to a foreign country—call it "crisis-land." We enter a new culture in which we are unsure of the proper behavior or etiquette. And just as every country honors and mourns the dead in its own ways, each person will grieve in his or her particular way. We understand that there is a universal language related to grief and loss, but we must still try to understand the specific needs and vocabulary of each survivor.

And don't forget the value of a sense of humor. Its importance cannot be overestimated.

We have all done it. Insert foot in mouth. The second the words come out, we cringe. Sometimes they're just silly bloopers, like the time I kept calling a friend whose mother had just died, could only get an answering machine, and finally blurted out, "*Hellooooo*, anyone home? I'm just looking for a *live body* over there." *Oops*. Or the first time I was interviewing a blind woman seeking help, and I say, "I'm so glad to see you, why don't you just follow me into the other room." *Oops*. Or the time I was in line for a sumptuous luncheon buffet with a colleague in a wheelchair and say, "I'm *paralyzed* by all the options." *Oops again*. After our house was burglarized, a neighbor came to say he was very sorry to hear the news. I answered, "At least we have our health." True, but not exactly the right thing to say to someone who has just completed radiation treatments for cancer. *Even bigger oops*. But no harm done. I've said the goofiest things, sometimes using turns of phrase I swear I never otherwise say. They just come out in the wash of crisis.

Most gaffes are just that—a mistake, a slip of the tongue from nervousness or inexperience. We don't mean any harm. The problem is that real harm can be done, even unwittingly, when we bring careless words or deeds into the area of another's pain. If we aren't careful, we can forever damage relationships, no matter how close we once were. Most of us, frankly, are never taught how to behave in the face of the deepest grief.

Individuals who have just been through a catastrophe are raw. It's as if their skin has been ripped off and nerve endings are exposed. We feel things times a thousand, and social interaction can be very painful. In the heat of the moment, our inner victim will even search for scapegoats—somewhere to target our rage. It's a strange thing, as if we need to take personal offense and be revictimized. Even the most well-meaning gesture can be suspect. "Why did they send these; they know I hate lilies!" Sound like a minefield? Not literally, but sort of. Given the importance of maintaining strong, healthy relationships, we need to learn how to proceed sensitively, even cautiously, in the face of another's duress.

What do survivors say has been helpful during their tough times? I call it "empathy etiquette"—the way to support survivors in crisis is by putting yourselves in their shoes. The good news is that we can learn empathy etiquette, much like we can learn resilience. When we are going through something for the first time, neither we nor our friends know exactly how to behave. Nothing seems normal or real in a life-threatening storm.

Emily Post, the etiquette guru, has some time-tested advice on this subject, particularly for families struggling with the death of a loved one. Brevity and practicality rule the etiquette path.

> Persons under the shock of genuine affliction are not only upset mentally but are all unbalanced physically. No matter how calm and controlled they seemingly may be, no one can, under such circumstances, be normal. Their disturbed circulation makes them cold, their distress makes them unstrung, sleepless. Persons they normally like, they often turn

from. No one should ever be forced upon those in grief, and all overemotional people, no matter how near or dear, should be barred absolutely. Although the knowledge that their friends love them and sorrow for them is a great solace, the nearest afflicted must be protected from any one or anything which is likely to overstrain nerves already at the threatening point, and none have the right to feel hurt if they are told they can neither be of use nor be received. At such a time, to some people companionship is a comfort, others shrink from dearest friends. One who is by choice or accident selected to come in contact with those in new affliction should, like a trained nurse, banish all consciousness of self; otherwise he or she will be of no service—and service is the only gift of value that can be offered.[4]

Etiquette is about making other people feel at ease. It requires a ruthless selflessness, just as Ms. Post advises: "Banish all consciousness of self." That's a tall order, particularly when none of us feels particularly at ease in the midst of a crisis. How do we check ourselves at the door, making comfort completely about others?

When I was young, I had no idea how to approach people in trouble—I either said nothing or the first things that came to mind. What to say to the parents of two high school classmates killed in a car crash senior year? (*I'm sorry, but were they drinking?*) What to say or do about a bulimia-induced rush to McLean Hospital in Boston, to keep a friend's weight from dipping below a skeletal eighty-four pounds? (*Can you please eat, for me?*) Or a neighbor's suicide attempt, requiring me to gather dishcloths and wait outside while my mother mopped up the razor-induced blood pools on a kitchen floor? (*Do you want some help with that?*) What about the gang rape of a classmate in

Rhode Island? (*Are you going to be okay tonight?*) Or the chronic fatigue visited upon an athletic friend? (*Do you think you might feel like playing tennis tomorrow?*) So many things were going wrong around me growing up, and no one was able to explain comprehensibly what to do or say.

When I was thirteen, the father of one of my best friends, Katie, rowed a dinghy offshore on a cold Thanksgiving weekend and shot himself in the head. It was the first time I heard the word *suicide*. The news kicked me in the gut. I didn't really understand what my parents were talking about. What was "manic depression," anyway? What did I know about helping my friend deal with her family's explosion?

My mother's demand that I go see Katie immediately made me choke up enough to feign illness. *Oh, no, what would I say?* I refused to get in the car. My mother said I didn't have to stay long or say much. "Just go knock on the door, ask for Katie, and say, 'I'm sorry.' That's all. Don't worry if you cry. Jerry, this is something you must learn to do. Katie needs you." (I learned much later in life that when my own mother was thirteen, none of her school friends had said a word when her own father, whom she adored, died unexpectedly from pneumonia.)

So I went to Katie's house. The place was eerily quiet. Katie turned the corner, pale in a tired way, and a little sheepish, "Hi, Jerry."

I averted my eyes, then gave her an abrupt hug. "I'm sorry about your dad." Katie looked down, whispered thanks and even smiled faintly.

This was the first date—a before-and-after moment—I remember sharing with a friend. At the time, I didn't understand why Katie said thanks. Now I do.

People at any age are relieved and grateful for simple gestures.

Now that I am older, I can appreciate my mother's early tutorial on condolences and life etiquette. I took from this formative experience two things: First, you must show up. Go to the place of suffering and be present. Second, keep your words simple and few: "I'm sorry."

Why is this so hard to do? Mainly because deep suffering is visceral and taps into our worst fears. It could happen to us. Thank God, it wasn't *my* husband who got hit by a car—or *my* wife who got the cancer diagnosis. We either want to run from it, fix it, or explain it away. We have to resist the temptations to do too much (*fix things*), to say too much (*overcompensate*), or to pretend too much (*acting as if nothing has really changed*).

It helps to think of grief with some detachment. Grief just is . . . an emotional fact. Some people talk a lot about it; others, not so much. The most important thing is to acknowledge grief without giving it permission to rule your life.

It may be disappointing, but many times people can't support us in the ways we want them to. Families are notorious on this front. No one can meet all our needs, nor read our minds. And sometimes the one person you want a hug from most is the very person who can't give it to you. Jeannie thinks she was too young to know how to ask for what she needed when her father died.

The date was May 22, 1976, five days before my thirteenth birthday. My mom picked me up from camp. As she put the car in park she simply said, "Dad died." I don't remember her hugging me, though I'm sure she must have. I don't remember her crying, though I'm sure she must have. I just remember going through a lot of Kleenex and really not being able to believe that someone who had always been there would never be there again.

Then the really hard part started. Because he had died the day before, all the relatives were already there, filling the house. Everyone was waiting for me, wanting to see my reaction. "How is she doing?" they whispered. "Can I hug you?" they asked. I went into my room and closed the door and cried some more. It seemed like every five minutes someone knocked. I was so polite and eager to please that I gave them all hugs and told them I was okay and thank you for coming.

An hour later, my youth pastor showed up to do her pastoral duty. She sat next to me in my darkened, cluttered room. She said, "You can cry." But I heard, "You should be crying." My head was throbbing from hours of crying. I wanted her to go away and I wanted to be alone and not cry. But I cried for her . . . hoping she'd be satisfied and feel good about herself and go away. My relatives seemed to think I was doing "well" if I wasn't crying. Hmmm, for an eager-to-please girl, it was getting hard to keep track of everyone's agendas for my grief.

My eldest brother showed up. He was twenty-two, getting his master's at Stanford. I was in the backyard, watching a litter of puppies we had. This was the hug I longed for with all my heart. Shouldn't he hug me? Doesn't he understand? But he just sat in a chair nearby and didn't say much. This moment, more than any other in my life, encapsulates the alienation and loneliness I felt in my family. Our father had just died, and we sat watching those puppies in silence.

I only wish we could rewind the clock and rewrite the script, whispering in Jeannie's brother's ear, *"Go ahead, reach out and hug your sister . . . just acknowledge her."* But that would have required him being able to think past his own emotional avalanche.

Paula's husband, David, was killed on September 11, 2001, in the terrorist attack on the World Trade Center in New York. She hadn't planned on raising three young sons as a single mom.

> I don't think of myself as a victim or survivor, per se. David is the victim here. He's the one who was killed . . . But I do know this is the hardest thing I have had to deal with in life, for sure—a before-and-after moment for my family. One of the things that strikes me looking back is how my neighbors became neighbors. It is not easy to reach out when you feel so needy. In fact, I resisted support at times because I couldn't handle any more people in my home, or all the phone calls. Many of the neighbors on my block I really didn't know so well before 9/11, but their kindness left an indelible impression that will be with me always.
>
> It's funny how I feel a little guilty when I see all the Tupperware in my cupboard—so many casseroles and goodies delivered to comfort me and my boys after the shock of losing David. I think I put on blinders at some point, just to get through, and now I can't recall all the kind gestures from so many. What would Miss Manners say about returning Tupperware and casserole dishes? How can I possibly repay so many, or write enough thank-you notes to show my gratitude? There's one gorgeous dish, with artistic detailing, someone left behind. I feel a tinge of guilt every time I use it, wondering whose it is. I've decided the best way for me to thank people is to pay their kindness forward to others in pain . . . to look for opportunities to show empathy and support. Because I've been comforted by the kindness of

strangers, I will do the same for others. I hope this ripple effect might help other hurting families who are facing profound loss. And, no, I don't want any of them to write me a thank-you or return "my" Tupperware. Who knows? It might be theirs after all.

Sometimes the most powerful gift we give is simple encouragement. After Debra lost her husband to a heart attack, she told me how grateful she was when other people who had been through tough times kept telling her, "You're going to be okay." Debra needed a house full of people, not quiet contemplation.

My daughter and I are blessed with the most loving and caring friends. They never left our side. They brought unconditional love and support to us and our immediate families. They truly did everything and anything for us. During the dark days after my husband's death, my daughter and I would lie on the bed in my room and listen to our friends reminisce about Herb. They filled our home and our hearts with love and laughter. They also filled our home with food, food, food and a full bar!

Just be ready to pick up on the hints people in crisis my give as to what is needed at any particular time. Try to make it about that person and not your own hang-ups or past traumas. Maybe your friend wants you to come by every day. Maybe it's just once a week. You must assess and reassess the situation. Be open. Be kind. Bring food. Then run the vacuum and wipe down the kitchen counters after putting the leftovers away in the fridge. After her miscarriage, my wife supplied our neighbor Beth with a steady stream of escapist books and funny movies.

When I was in the throes of it, I read an entire bag of Kelly's romance novels. They transported me away from my problems to another place and time, where everything ends happily. They were a fantastic way to get away from it all without leaving my room. I watched *Notting Hill* about ten times. Same deal. It's funny, it's a love story; there are beautiful people and delightful accents, and everyone is happy at the end. It's what my mother the librarian refers to as "brain candy." I think it's the best thing for a heartache.

The harder the situation, the more the family will appreciate your presence and support. You do not need to make lengthy visits—sometimes a few minutes will suffice. But your willingness to go out of your way to say a few words of comfort will never be forgotten.

Studies show that people most often offer advice and words of reassurance as common expressions of sympathy to people going through loss. But, survivors themselves will tell you, advice and assurance are the *least* helpful. Supportive listening is the *most* helpful. Even when people don't want to talk, your job is still to listen. Don't fill the air with words. Don't pry or ask too many questions. When you are initially at a loss for words, however, here are some appropriate icebreakers.

I'm sorry.

Thank you for letting me know.

How are you doing with all this?

I'm here to support you in whatever you need.

What's the hardest part for you?

I'll call you tomorrow.

How are you coping?

Take the time you need.

Thank you for sharing your feelings.

The etiquette of consoling is about learning to communicate genuine affection and unconditional acceptance. It's never too late to start. Here are several condolence tips drawn from survivor experience:

- **Acknowledge our loss.** Even saying the "wrong" thing sincerely is better than saying nothing at all. Try something like, "I'm not sure what to say, but I'm sorry for what happened, and I really care." If you feel you've said something insensitive, it's better to acknowledge it outright: "I'm sorry, that was probably the wrong thing to say. I just want to help."
- **Look for specific ways to offer help.** Well-meaning friends often say, "Please let me know if there's anything I can do." Such an invitation puts the burden on us to think of something and then "assign" it. Unlikely. Try instead, "I will call you Tuesday morning to drive you to the appointment." Then do it.
- **Pitch in.** Handling mundane chores provides welcome relief during stressful times. It allows us to focus on urgent needs and tend to our loved ones, not just things on the task list. If a friend is spending all her time at the hospital with her ailing father, offer to pick the kids up from school, shovel the driveway, walk the dog, or shop for groceries. Every bit helps. But try to give graciously and anonymously, if you can, without waiting for recognition or a special thank you.
- **Talk about the person who died and use their name.** You can do this whether they just passed away or have been gone for years. When friends and relatives avoid all mention of a dead person, it is as if their life

has been erased, and this is even more painful than the loss itself.

- **Share your memories.** It is always nice to jot down a memory and give it to the family. You don't have to wait for a holiday to do so. Also, if you think your friend's late husband would have been proud of their daughter's recent music performance or graduation, share that sentiment. Even if you didn't know the person who died, ask about him or her.
- **Remember anniversaries and other significant days.** People often feel especially lonely on the anniversaries of tragic events, and also on holidays when families reminisce. If you think a particular day might be difficult for a friend or relative, offer to spend time with them on that day or send a card or e-mail to say you are thinking of them and remembering their loved one.
- **Continue to invite us to special occasions.** If we have recently experienced a loss, we may need some encouragement to get out and socialize. At first we may decline, but that doesn't mean we don't appreciate the invitation. Bereavement is painful enough, but no one wants to lose their connection with normal life and friends in the process.[5]

Empathy etiquette is about being keenly observant and caring. The general purpose is to make others feel more comfortable. It's not about you. It's about them. Offering help is never wrong, and in most cases our common sense will guide us. As long as we keep reminding ourselves that no matter what, our friend or the survivor comes first—not the illness, not the crutch, not the doctor, not even the crisis. If you ever have a question—what to do, how to do it, how to say it—the survivor will always be your best resource. You can ask.

The last thing anyone needs is pity. Friedrich Nietzsche put his finger on it: "Pity stands opposed to the tonic emotions which heighten our vitality: it has a depressing effect. We are deprived of strength when we feel pity."[6] I couldn't agree more that pity encourages victimhood by sapping a survivor's resilience. Pity implies that a person is a bit pathetic and lacks the capacity to cope. Sympathy is only mildly better, defined as "a feeling or expression of sorrow for the distress of another; commiseration."[7] While sympathy may not be as demoralizing as pity, it falls short of helpful. Sympathy is what we find in greeting cards when others hear we are going through something difficult. Knowing someone cares is better than nothing, but sympathy implies some distance, and on its own will not do much to build up and encourage a survivor. What is called for in crisis is compassion and empathy in action. You feel for and with someone in pain; you show you care; you show up, watch your tongue, and offer practical support.

In Job, the oldest book of the Bible, we find the story of a kindly God-fearing gentleman abused by Satan and assaulted verbally by his friends and neighbors. A true survivor, Job will not tolerate pity or abide sympathy from anyone. Instead, he demands truth and justice. In the Book of Job we discover timeless counsel on the dos and don'ts of approaching people in the midst of their personal plague. Job's three friends start off well enough when confronted with Job's massive misfortune. They keep silent. But after only a week, they can't resist opening their mouths. *What had Job done to deserve this calamity? Maybe he wasn't as righteous as everyone thought?* Classic blame-the-victim stuff. Ultimately, their judgmental misreading of the situation triggers an angry rebuke from Job:

If you and I were to change places, I could talk like you; how I could harangue you and wag my head at you! But no, I would speak words of encouragement, and then my condolences would flow in streams. If I speak, my pain is not eased; if I am silent, it does not leave me. Meanwhile, my friend wearies me with false sympathy . . . [8]

God demonstrates tough love with His thunderous voice out of the tempest, but He also shows some good empathy etiquette. To begin with, He waits a *very* long time—thirty-seven chapters—before speaking. Unlike Job's fair-weather friends, God took time to listen. And when God does speak, He lets these friends know they were not helpful to Job. *"When the Lord had finished speaking to Job, He said to Eliphaz the Temanite, 'I am angry with you and your two friends, because you have not spoken as you ought about me, as my servant Job has done.'"*[9]

Job begged for mercy, but he never gave up. He got plenty mad, with grief and unanswered questions, but he didn't concede hope that if he could just hear from God, things might get better. And even if they didn't, Job would at least have had his day in court. After the worst suffering a person can endure—death of family, loss of livelihood, chronic pain and illness, reduced to living on the streets—Job goes on to thrive. *"The Lord blessed the end of Job's life more than the beginning . . . He had seven sons and three daughters . . . He saw his sons and his grandsons to four generations, and died at a very great age."*[10]

In the end, aren't we all "put in our place" by disaster and death? Life can hurt us terribly, and our deepest questions are never fully answered. We, like Job, will never know *why* we're allowed to be tortured by fate. But if we hang on long enough, we will see there is a sequel in survivorship—the opportunity for us to grow stronger and thrive.

In sum, when it comes to empathy etiquette, Job's friends would have done well to remember some basic guidelines drawn from survivor experience:

- Don't blame victims or feel sorry for them. Respect their strength; empathy requires dignity, not pity.
- Don't try to fix or rescue people. Offer support instead of advice.
- Don't talk too much. Listen and try open-ended questions.
- Don't pretend things are the same. Acknowledge the situation.
- When you visit, make yourself helpful.

On our trip to Bosnia in 1997, shortly before her death, Diana, Princess of Wales, would insist the most important thing was "caring enough to show up" and always remembering to say "thank you" any time someone has welcomed you into their home or shared a piece of their lives. Two weeks later, I honored her by attending her funeral and simply telling her two sons how much she loved them and talked about them nonstop during that last summer. "I know, she told me all about her trip," Prince William said quietly as his blue eyes glanced downward, a mirror image of his mother. "Thank you," he added. "My mother loved people." I didn't try to say anything else, just a nod.

It was Princess Diana, after my own mother, who taught me the most about holding steady, with dignity, in the presence of another's suffering. Diana had the gift. And she was able to develop her skills over the years, during visit after visit to hospitals, hospices, and homeless shelters. Yes, it takes practice.

By listening to others pour out their grief (while minding our manners), we are able to nudge people who are suffering onto their path of survivorship. That's all we can do for them. Whether or not they go on to thrive? Well, that's up to them, isn't it?

11

SURVIVE. INSPIRE. THRIVE!

◆

Obviously, I believe in the power of the human spirit to overcome fear and tragedy. I've seen it so many times that I am
convinced each and every one of us possesses the power to
transform ourselves after life explodes. We can discover in our
scar tissue something meaningful, even beautiful. That is, if
we *choose* to do so. And we must, if we want to fulfill our potential and thrive.

On April 12, 1984, that landmine stole a part of my leg, but
not *me*. I never gave it the power to make me less than whole,
less than who I am. I've learned that nothing is big enough to do
that. Nothing can eradicate joy and peace forever, unless we allow it. True, we can be victimized and changed in an instant.
Something terrible comes to our door through no fault of our
own. But we can find strength and purpose in our hour of need.
This journey to overcome is both what makes us human, and
what makes us whole.

I have filled this book with stories of individuals who have
evolved through struggle. None is perfect. No one ever com-

pletely arrives. But even survivors *en route* to thriving inspire us to get up off our victim couches and get busy living and loving others.

The biggest challenge in my work is to get people unstuck from the patterns of victimhood—coaching them to let go of the ghosts of their past and reach for a more positive future. There will always be victimization and tragedy, of course. But I believe the world could be a healthier, more peaceful place if more and more people were able to overcome adversity by using the five basic steps: face facts, choose life, reach out, get moving, and give back.

For some to start on this path, all it takes is a simple invitation or kick in the pants from a friend they trust. For others, it takes more time, sensitivity, and practical support, supplied by a mentor, relative, or coach. For many, it's just about the opportunity to participate—a chance to work, to contribute and belong. One survivor told me his breakthrough "aha" moment came the first time he watched someone play wheelchair basketball. *Hey, I could do that!*

Having a role model can mean the difference between success and failure. Maybe that's why we often turn people into heroes. We need to. And some well-known or iconic survivors just fit the bill. Like survivors of the Holocaust.

When I met Elie Wiesel for the first time, he struck me as more than a survivor. He's an inspirer who speaks and writes the language of resilience. He was born in 1928 in Sighet, a largely Jewish town taken over by the Nazis in 1944, when all Jews, including his family, were sent to concentration camps. Wiesel wrote of his experience in *Night*, one of the most frequently read stories to emerge from the Holocaust.[1] He was awarded the 1986 Nobel Prize for Peace for speaking out against violence, repression, and racism, but Wiesel never ceases to affirm our need to pursue grace in our lives, wherever and whenever we can:

> We know that every moment is a moment of grace, every hour an offering; not to share them would mean to betray them. Our lives no longer belong to us alone; they belong to all those who need us desperately.[2]

I think grace, in part, is what allows survivors to bring meaning to our stories. It's available to all of us—moments of awakening. Without meaning, you may survive, but you will never inspire. And without meaning, you cannot ultimately thrive. Finding meaning in our lives is a way to dispel darkness and break through the barriers that imprison us. As Friedrich Nietzsche observed, "He who has a *why* to live for can bear with almost any *how*."

Helen Keller and her teacher Anne Sullivan exemplify thriver personalities. Sullivan came from poverty, was visually impaired, and at age twenty became Helen's tutor. Keller went on to accomplish more in her life as a blind and deaf woman than many people achieve with the use of all physical faculties. She demonstrated a remarkable determination to overcome fear, conquering the things that once terrified her. Whenever tempted to feel sorry for herself, she made a point to push aside self-pity and chose life. I think her 1903 Radcliffe College essay, "Optimism," is a classic for people aiming to thrive.

> Once I knew the depth where no hope was, and darkness lay on the face of all things. Then love came and set my soul free. Once I knew only darkness and stillness. Now I know hope and joy. Once I fretted and beat myself against the wall

that shut me in. Now I rejoice in the consciousness that I can think, act and attain heaven.[3]

Hope. Joy. Love. Freedom. These are attributes of a thriving personality. Thrivers who survive threatening conditions report feeling transformed by their experience—from dark to light, from imprisonment to freedom. Yet they shrug off any mention of heroism or courage. They say anyone in the same circumstances would do the same. But that is not true. Not everyone bounces back and resumes life with new energy. Thrivers do. We watch them return to everyday life stronger than before, more confident, more spiritual, wiser.

What is their secret? Determination, combined with dignity and the support of others.

Ms. Keller describes a childhood experience in which she climbed a tree with her teacher, Anne Sullivan, and then remained there alone while Ms. Sullivan went to retrieve some lunch from the house. While she sat there, a storm began to gather. She had no idea if anyone was near and could not get down from the tree herself. She describes the scene as being one of the first times that she came to appreciate the inherent danger in life and experience the feeling of pure vulnerability and fear. Yet the following spring, she found the aroma of a blooming mimosa tree so beautiful and enticing that she overcame her fears and climbed it by herself. Later, she considered it one of the most heavenly places she knew, and spent much time as a kid in this tree and many others.[4]

For thrivers, bravery comes not from being unafraid, but rather from recognizing the fear and facing it head-on. Keller knew the forest hosted too much beauty and pleasure to avoid it. She moved out of her comfort zone and in for the embrace.

Can we be like Keller? Like Wiesel? Like others who determine to thrive? I believe we *all* possess the kernels of a thriver. It is within all of us to overcome—with purpose, with meaning, with energy.

Sometimes we put survivors on pedestals, making superheroes out of them, in real life as well as fiction. Even I do it. I read and reread biographies and biblical stories, seeking inspiration. But I'm certainly not above a dip into pop culture. Take Spider-Man, for example. You may recall the story of Peter Parker: He attends a science exhibition where he is bitten by a radioactive spider. The bite gives Peter an array of powers, including wall-crawling, superstrength, speed, and agility, not to mention an extrasensory "spider sense." Peter initially sets out to cash in on his mutant gifts, seeking fame and fortune. But after a TV appearance, he allows a thief to escape the station, thinking, it's "not my problem." The same burglar subsequently kills his uncle Ben. Realizing he could have prevented his uncle's death, Peter commits to a life of crime fighting and lifesaving, driven by his uncle's words, *"With great power there must also come great responsibility."* This motto forms the basis of Spider-Man's moral core (as it does for many on the survivor path), learning that survivorship is about more than ourselves. He strives to do what's right for the community, even as he's vilified by some skeptical observers.

When I first started campaigning to ban landmines, I empathized with Spider-Man. Though I didn't have a costume or comic book, I became obsessed with fighting the weapon that had "bitten" me years earlier. It had made me different. And it literally haunted my dreams as I worked around the clock to eradicate its effects. It took three years for me to work it out of my system, to heal and let go. I realized my life wasn't about a weapon—the thing that had taken my leg. It was about people.

And my work was really about survivors helping others to overcome their personal dates with disaster. It was about giving people the basic mental and physical tools they need to let go of the past and get on with their lives.

I have had the privilege to work with heroes of all types, some just struggling to survive, and others serving and leading their communities. So who is a hero, really? The late Christopher Reeve nails it in his autobiography:

> When the first *Superman* movie came out, I gave dozens of interviews to promote it. The most frequently asked question was, "What is a hero?" I remember how easily I had talked about it, the glib response I repeated so many times. My answer was that a hero is someone who commits a courageous action without considering the consequences . . . And I also meant individuals who are slightly larger than life . . . who have taken on mythical proportions. Now my definition is completely different. I think a hero is an ordinary individual who finds the strength to persevere and endure in spite of overwhelming obstacles.[5]

That's where you and I come in. We don't always have to look for larger-than-life heroes. We can be heroes for each other. We are just ordinary folk wanting to endure and live life well, even during the rough patches. But we can all benefit from role models who not only overcome adversity, but find the wherewithal to give back and serve the broader community. This is how we complete the cycle of survivorship, transforming our tragedy and blessing others in the process.

Colleen is one of my survivor heroes—a tough cookie with a sweet laugh. I mentioned her earlier; she had the father who came home from Korea and terrorized his family. Today,

Colleen thinks of herself as a thriver, not just a survivor, but it was not always so. She had to learn how to think through her past, rather than let it hold her hostage.

When I was six, my sister and I were playing with our best friends, who were twins. One of the twins ran out into the street and was hit by a truck, killed in front of our eyes. My sister never bounced back from that day. I think she had been weakened by the abuse she had already endured in her short life. It was the opposite for me. I don't know why exactly, but when our friend died, I remember being really upset and crying, but then thinking, "Wow, I guess that's how life is; you are here one minute and gone the next."

For me, these childhood experiences were like rings in my tree stump, with many other rings coming later. I believe my sister, on the other hand, made our childhood experiences like the branches and leaves on her tree of life. They defined her. Sadly, she couldn't see anything else. The stories became her life, and she couldn't seem to get past the past. It became a cancer that slowly ate away inside her until, at thirty-five, she died of cancer.

What do I take away from these tragedies? Well, early on in life I found out what I was made of. I like that part. I count on it. Though I wouldn't wish it on anyone, I am stronger because of it. I have learned to use my "tragedy-gift" as a reference point—my personal GPS [Global Positioning System] in life. I have also come to believe there are two ways people tend to see the world. Life is a pie and I have to get the biggest slice I can. That's one way to survive—to fight for it. Or we can see life as a pie that we can help to make bigger. That is what I ask of myself. How can I make my life bigger than this one thing?

Was surviving all that horrible stuff in my past meaningful? Yes, I think so. I have come to believe that you can reframe any situation, put it in context, and talk about what happens to you in the way you choose. Looking at the past is a narrow prism, but looking at the life we have ahead of us is expansive. I tell people all the time that you will find what you are looking for.

None of the survivors interviewed in this book would call themselves heroes, or particularly courageous, for that matter. They simply did what they had to do. They dug deep and, like Colleen, found what they were looking for.

I think also of heroic Helen, who has lost her eyesight in her nineties. She is adamant that we rediscover our inner strength.

I remember when a young boy died in the fifth grade. His name was Vincent. It was sad, and we kids talked about it a lot, and our parents did, but no one brought in counselors or stopped school. People did talk about things back then, but maybe not in the same way. Many more people in my generation found help in traditional religion—some daily rituals to help sustain us in good times and bad.

I'm afraid we're not as resourceful as we could be. People seem to be looking for help everywhere outside themselves. There are all these counselors for everything, even in the elementary schools. Almost every kid I hear about today has an acronym attached to his or her name—ADD, LD, maybe even a Ph.D., for all I know. We didn't have all that growing up. We had to find our way without relying on experts all the time. We had no "shrinks" or psychologists hanging out at our schools and neighborhoods growing up, not that I was aware of. But things change, and I don't want to sound old-fashioned. I welcome all the help we can get, and I'm truly grateful for it.

I would just like to see us rediscover some of our inner strength, and maybe chatter a bit less about all our personal troubles. I've actually lived through the Depression and too many wars. I think we need to work together on the very real problems of the world, like peace.

Helen is on to something. *Perspective*. It is gained from her nine decades of living through ups and downs. She understands the paradox that on the one hand we can't predict all the storms life will bring, but on the other hand we must in fact prepare for the storms that come our way. That's where resilience comes in. We must build it for ourselves and our families. These days, it seems, Americans are much less prepared for trials and tribulations than, say, the so-called Greatest Generation who survived World War II. Or maybe we are becoming desensitized from twenty-four-hour media coverage of crime, corruption, and global violence. Could it be that we are raising our children in America to become the least resilient and least resourceful generation in history? It is important to remind ourselves and to teach our kids that there is a real difference between minor afflictions and real tragedy. And by learning to handle the lesser challenges well, as we grow, we can prepare for the bigger ones to come.

I suggest we learn from those who have gone before us, like Helen. The healthy survivor types are easy to spot. They are the people living in the community, often older, going about their lives, not wearing their trauma on their sleeves. These survivors become role models of resilience and agents for positive change. They tend to think of others more than themselves, and give more than they get.

These individuals who go beyond basic survival and learn to give back reveal what I call a thriver personality. One doesn't detect any bitterness or resentment in their speech or actions. They have clearly moved on from their catastrophe. They embrace the whole crazy quilt of life—the good and the bad. They go that extra mile to make this world better, but don't expect a trophy. Take a moment to think of someone you know who seems to thrive in your community. Why is it? Believe me, it's not his or her good looks or money. It's attitude. It's a mind-set.

Thrivers are all around us, not distant in history or geography. They are most often applied optimists. Pessimists can also thrive, but they have to work a bit harder to push through their tendency toward negativity. Similarly, introverts sometimes find it harder to thrive than extroverts, given the need to reach out for support during and after a crisis. The key is to know yourself so you can work with or compensate for your natural tendencies.

You recall the story of Kathryn, an incest and abuse survivor who used to deal drugs in Connecticut, but now helps people living with HIV/AIDS in Africa.

When I was a drug dealer, I used to drive around at night and look into people's living rooms. They all seemed so happy, and I was very unhappy. When I got sober, I still felt ashamed of who I was. I beat myself up more than anyone. I looked better on the outside but was still dying on the inside. Even when I learned the lingo of AA, I thought I was a fraud. It felt like I learned to live the "façade"—but who was the real me? Then a friend said to me, "Kathryn, lighten up, you are not just playing the façade—you really are that person and it's a wonderful person."

I am no longer afraid. In fact, I remember very well the first moment I wasn't afraid. I was thirty-three years old driving in my car. It suddenly occurred to me that I felt comfortable in my own skin. What a great feeling! To no longer feel scared and ashamed. That's why no one can hurt or control me anymore. Being a survivor makes me feel strong.

Thriver personalities have been tested. They are intimately acquainted with their own imperfections and vulnerability. But they, like Kathryn, emerge "comfortable in their own skin." They are able to summon the courage to affirm the best life has to offer, in spite of the temptation to backslide and despair.

I think again of Elizabeth, the godmother of my son. She's smart and self-assured—graceful. You'd never know she'd been through traumatic family conflict, here and abroad, as well as the death of a baby and her husband. You'd just think, "What a lovely, insightful woman." But insight is born from experience. Elizabeth points to Psalm 84 for a clue to her survivor inspiration. She says these words have been important throughout her life:

Blessed are those whose strength is in Thee,
Who have set their hearts on pilgrimage.
As they pass through the Valley of Baca,
They make it a place of springs . . .
(Psalm 84:5-6)

The Valley of Baca is a reference to a place of weeping, a parched valley of desolation. I think of Baca as the place of our greatest trial and hardship. Elizabeth reflects further on her own life's pilgrimage:

> If we can accept that life is a journey and not insist that things remain static or controllable—if we can accept the discomforts of the pilgrimage, finding our strength in God and trusting that He is with us, then we are able to make dry places into wells. The psalm writer is clear that as we pass through these difficulties, there is an option, there is something we can do as we suffer. We can turn these hardships into blessings, into places of refreshment, of springs. We will be able to find grace and patience and ultimately satisfaction as we see our situations turn around. A dear friend, Hannah, used to tell me that the trick was to live long enough to see all the good which God intended for our lives come into fruition.

To thrive takes time and perspective, but it's doable. You need patience. Most of us are a work in progress—survivors *en route*. Make no mistake about it: thrivers live all around us. It's just that most of them don't advertise it on their sleeves. Like Elizabeth, we can observe them tending their own garden, giving out in quiet ways, with compassion, not compulsion. We note their kindness and their time for other people. Despite the trauma they've been through, they become less self-absorbed and more giving.

One of my all-time favorite thrivers in the Bible is Joseph, of multicolored-coat fame. Joseph was all about thriving after trouble. Despite his brothers' jealousy and cruelty, he determined to make the best of his lot, even after losing his princely life, being most favored by his father, Jacob. Time and again, Joseph was brought down, unfairly punished, because of other people's weaknesses. But each time he did the best he could to "make wells" in very trying circumstances. Joseph grew through adversity, choosing to forgive and then move forward. Each of his decisions to overcome the past and choose life laid the very foundation that prepared him for a future of influence and importance. What if Joseph had pouted, preferred revenge, and stayed a victim? He would not have been able to step right out of jail into a position of prominence at the palace, where he advised the Pharaoh, saving all of Egypt and his own people.

Sounds a bit like Nelson Mandela in South Africa, doesn't it? Some thrivers, like Mandela, are historically iconic, of biblical proportions. They serve as universal role models. I for one will never forget February 11, 1990, the date Nelson Mandela walked free from Robben Island after twenty-eight years in prison. Body erect. Dignity intact. Grace in motion. He wrote in his memoirs:

> I am fundamentally an optimist. Whether that comes from nature or nurture, I cannot say. Part of being optimistic is keeping one's head pointed toward the sun, one's feet moving forward. There were many dark moments when my faith in humanity was sorely tested, but I would not and could not give myself up to despair. That way lay defeat and death.[6]

Thrivers don't give in to despair, at least not for long. They struggle. They Face Facts, but then Get Moving as well. They break through barriers and emerge stronger. They then honor their good fortune by finding ways to Give Back—by gratefully helping their peers.

I have been blessed to work with and meet many remarkable survivor teachers over the years. In December 2001, for example, the Nobel Committee invited all past winners of the Peace Prize to Norway for a weekend retreat to discuss peace. I was invited as one of the leaders of the International Campaign to Ban Landmines, co-recipient of the 1997 Peace Prize. I shared breakfast, lunch, and dinner, lectures and discussion groups, with the likes of Desmond Tutu, Elie Wiesel, Lech Walesa, Oscar Arias, and other laureates.

One of the intriguing ironies of the weekend was that no one could quite agree how best to describe peace. We all agreed, though, that it's not just the absence of conflict. That's too simple and expresses peace as a negative. Laureate Rigoberta Menchú proposed ripe fruit as the apt metaphor. Rigoberta was raised in the Quiche branch of the Mayan culture in Guatemala. Her father, mother, and brother were all arrested, abused, and killed by government security forces for allegedly participating in guerrilla activities on behalf of the peasant population in Guatemala. Rigoberta became a passionate advocate for indigenous rights and reconciliation, not only in Guatemala but in the Western Hemisphere generally. During our time together, she mentioned an indigenous word that is used to describe a piece of fruit on a tree just before it is picked or falls to the ground. It is round and juicy, full and complete. Yes, to me, that's more like peace.

When we are most at peace, our inside and outside are aligned. We are in balance. I suggested to the group that thriving is a kind of peace. It brings that fullness and balance we need, inside and out, for you and me; for individuals and communities. Just think for a moment of the most calm or passionate thriver you know; then imagine communities full of people like him or her. Picture that world—abundant, peaceful, creative.

As the weekend wrapped up, I found myself talking to His Holiness the Dalai Lama. I asked him about his concept of karma and peace. I wondered why so many wounded people around the world believed they had bad karma. Did he truly think disability and misfortune were the result of their misdeeds in a past life? His Holiness smiled and pulled my head onto his shoulder, saying, *"There is no 'us' and 'them.' There is no 'we' and 'they.' All are one."*

I wasn't exactly sure whether he had answered my question, but I was struck silent by the simplicity of his message. It went inside me, not just through my ears. Suffering. Triumph. It is all to be shared. It joins us all.

I immediately thought back to Cambodia, where years earlier the young girl with one leg had said to me, "You are one of us." *Yes, I am. All are one.* We are all connected in our sorrows and our joys—in our mutual survivorship on this planet.

There is much at stake. Embracing the patterns of victimhood has cost the human race a great deal. Headlines of terrorism, violence, and disaster assault us with increasing frequency. And the mass of victims grows daily. Individuals blame one another. Communities put up walls. Nations blame nations. How can we turn the victim tide, reaching out to the growing number of hurting individuals, providing the hope and support they need to transform into survivors who seek to fulfill their potential, who aspire to thrive? Can we help ourselves do the same? Will we start reaching out to others, connecting our hardship and theirs? It takes courage and a lot of hard work to turn the tide. It requires letting go of past resentments and bitterness. It means moving forward. I hope, by our example, we

can help the world do likewise, building a future with survivors united.

We won't get very far without first looking in the mirror
and taking full responsibility for our own survivor trek. We
might have to sit down with pen and paper to chart the facts of
our lives—marking the dates of sorrow and joy—with notes
on the ups and downs of emotion and evolving relationships.
Keep in mind all the survivors throughout history who have
marked the way. Their survivor compass, using the five steps,
will help guide us.

Our dates with disaster are not over. We will get knocked
to the ground again. But there, with our senses assaulted, we
will notice things we never noticed before. I think of one of
our national before-and-after moments—September 11. I
hope it has not further propelled us into a culture of fear and
retribution. Fear is the twin of victimhood and the enemy of
survivorship, both individually and collectively. Only if we can
put fear behind us can we live fully. That is not to say there
aren't things *to* fear in this world. Terrorist attacks are meant to
terrify. But that doesn't mean we should live trapped *in* fear.

Though we don't ever fully "recover" from devastation
and loss, we can and must integrate our toughest experiences
and move on. Different, but still able to say yes to life. Recall
the story of Persephone being pulled into the underworld. She
never fully comes back, but her life is certainly full. The sheltered daughter of Zeus and Demeter, Persephone lives a
peaceful life until one day, innocently picking flowers with her
nymph playmates, the earth opens up and devours her. Hades,
god of the dead, has burst through a cleft in the earth to
abduct Persephone to become his underground queen. Zeus
eventually negotiates the release of his daughter, and things
get better, but they are never the same. Before Hades lets

Persephone go, he makes her eat pomegranate seeds, so she cannot stay away forever. Part of each year she must return underground, since she has eaten from its depth.

I remember well the feeling of eating dirt in a minefield. Life never quite tasted the same. I think if we pick up treasures there in the underworld or in the dirt and integrate them, part of us will always belong to that other place. We may miss our earlier innocence—before our date—when life was simpler, God was simpler, and relationships were simpler. But we must eschew a victim mentality and teach our peers and our children to tap into the positive power of a survivor society. We follow in the steps of survivors, aspiring to thrive.

Why, with what I've seen, do I still believe fiercely in life's possibility and potential? Am I just an idealist? Yes, proudly so. I possess a deep-rooted optimism and faith in people and the universe. I know we can all do better, be better, choose better. So why don't we? There's absolutely nothing special about me. The survivors you met in this book prove the point and the potential and resilience of the human spirit—your spirit. It's all about choices, matched by determination to survive well.

The Five Steps on our survivor journey offer a way not just to recover, not just to survive, but to thrive. Step by step, we find power to convert our dates—the days that change us—to become *more* than we were before the illness or the accident. We understand survivorship is anything but linear: it's a process that involves three steps forward, a flashback or two, and then a leap ahead. Each of us is a mixed breed of survivor and victim. One day we can exhibit healthy survivor behavior and then reveal less attractive victim behavior the next. No one is perfectly resilient or consistent. But we progress, day by day, step by step, if we want.

Like Mandela, always remember to keep your face turned toward the sun.

Strength and purpose are yours.

Face Facts. Choose Life. *Reach Out.* Get Moving. *Give Back.* Be inspired and thrive.

It's your choice.

ACKNOWLEDGMENTS

◆

No one survives nor succeeds alone, as we say in the survivor movement. It takes a community. And I have been blessed with a global one, with friends and teachers across many countries and cultures. Otherwise, this book would not be possible. I am indebted to and inspired by survivors of all types who have shared their personal stories with courage, poignancy, and even humor.

I am grateful to a handful of people who prevailed upon me to start documenting my experiences and recording my thoughts on surviving. Foremost is my wife, Kelly White. She was the first to encourage me to start writing down my recipe for resilience, drawing from years of survivor conversations. There would be no book without her support. There were two other provocateurs, Lekha Singh and Mary Daly, who were adamant that the time had come to communicate survivorship beyond the realm of war to a broader audience. Then there's the brilliant Erica Taylor, so fast and generous with her wisdom-crackling feedback. Last but not least, my heartfelt gratitude goes to the late Diana, Princess of Wales, who taught me about holding steady in the face of chaos and suffering. I would neither have started nor completed this project without a loving push from these catalytic women.

And who wouldn't be grateful for the gifted editors and the publishing team at St. Martin's Press? Thank you, Charlie Spicer and Yaniv Soha, for coaching me to discipline my narrative voice and offering editorial insight each step of the way. Even better, you believed this book was important, hoping it will touch many lives. Then there's David Kuhn, possibly the smartest, fastest agent-editor-advisor ever. He set me up right from the get-go. And with the perseverance of my exceptionally talented research assistant, Elizabeth Miner (and early support from intern Nicola Dougherty), we plowed through stacks of interview transcripts and survivor literature. The team kept me on task and we survived admirably well together. I hope the effort was successful, but if there are any mistakes, they're all mine.

My acknowledgments could easily grow longer than this short book, naming people who, whether they realize it or not, have opened doors of understanding and support. I've been inspired by the biblical Job, Joseph, and Jesus and modern-day saints like Jane Olson, a visionary leader and co-chair of Survivor Corps. She honored my need for space by recommending a three-month sabbatical to write. I couldn't have done it without her support and that of our calm and collected chief operating officer, Kristan Beck; our supreme survivor staff worldwide; and our mission-driven patrons and international board: Her Majesty Queen Noor of Jordan, The Honourable Hilary Weston, Peter Armitage, Richard Barker, Terry Berkemeier, Lincoln Bloomfield Jr., Louis Burnett, Ann Daniel, Fred Giuffrida, Carolyn Katz, Doug McCormack, Dee Dee

Myers, Caroline Pfohl-Ho, Ken Rutherford, Vin Ryan, Lionel Sauvage, Ivan Schouker, Ross Sherbrooke, Gail Snetro-Plewman, John Taylor, Bill Toliver, and Rick White.

More than a hundred survivors from more than a dozen countries contributed to this book. I wanted to include each and every voice. Alas, that was not possible, but I was able to learn from each, and select many gems from their experiences fundamental to the book's message. Given the sensitivity of some material and respect for privacy, I have cited only first names or initials and in three instances changed the name to honor the survivors' request for anonymity. I thank each and every survivor who contributed. Your willingness to share yourself is a gift. To hear more from these survivors, and add your voice to theirs if you wish, visit **http://www.survivor corps.org.**

Recognizing how our families sustain us, I acknowledge gratefully the support of my children, Kate, Quincy, Bo, and Jay; my siblings, Lisa, Rick, Susan, Ron, and Nick; my ever-supportive father, Allan White, now deceased; and my ever-cheering mother, Mimi White, whose loving voice is clear in the book.

Last but not least, I thank *you* for seeking to understand the secrets of survivorship, and then passing them along to others.

I wish peace and thriving upon you all.

To connect and share your ideas and experiences with people like you, please join us at **www.IWillNotBeBroken.com.**

If you are a survivor of war or conflict, or would like to support Jerry's ongoing fight on behalf of survivors of conflict, then join Survivor Corps at **www.survivorcorps.org.**

NOTES

◆

1. Everyone Has a Date with Disaster

1. Gillian A. King et al., eds., *Resilience: Learning from People with Disabilities and the Turning Points in their Lives* (Westport, CT: Praiger, 2003), 35.
2. Christopher Reeve, *Still Me* (New York and Toronto: Random House, 1998), 121.

3. Step 1: Face Facts

1. Zainab Salbi and Laurie Buckland, *Between Two Worlds—Escape from Tyranny: Growing Up in the Shadow of Saddam* (New York: Penguin, 2005), 5.
2. Ibid., 231.
3. Surya Das, *Letting Go of the Person You Used to Be: Lessons on Change, Loss and Spiritual Transformation* (New York: Broadway, 2003), 10–11.

4. Step 2: Choose Life

1. Christopher Reeve, *Still Me*, 33.
2. Norman B. Anderson and Elizabeth P. Anderson, *Emotional Longevity: What Really Determines How Long You Live* (New York: Penguin, 2004).
3. American Psychological Association, "Mind/Body Health," APA Practice Media Room, May 25, 2007, http://apahelpcenter.mediaroom.com/index.php?s—edia_library.
4. Ibid.

5. Step 3: Reach Out

1. A. E. Kazak and D. A. Christakis, "Caregiving issues in families of children with chronic medical conditions," *Family Caregiver Applications Series: Volume 4; Family Caregiving Across the Lifespan*, eds. E. Kahana, D. E. Biegel, and M. L. Wykle (Thousand Oaks, California: Sage, 1994), 331–355.
2. Christopher Reeve, *Still Me*, 47.
3. Daniel Goleman, "Religious Faith and Social Activity Help to Heal, New Research Finds," *New York Times,* February 4, 1995, late edition, 1:10.
4. John McCain, *Faith of My Fathers* (New York: HarperCollins, 2000), 309.
5. Ibid., 235.
6. Ibid., 308.
7. Steven A. Holmes, "James Stockdale, Perot's Running Mate in '92, Dies at 81," *New York Times*, July 6, 2005.
8. John McCain, 318.
9. Myra Glajchen and R. Magen, "Evaluating Process, Outcome, and Satisfaction in Community-Based Cancer Support Groups," *Support Groups: Current Perspectives on Theory and Practice*, ed. M. J. Galinsky and J. H. Schopler (New York: Haworth Press, 1996), 27–40.
10. S.L. Berman et al., "The Impact of Exposure to Crime and Vi-

olence on Urban Youth," *American Journal of Orthopsychiatry* 66, no. 3 (1996): 329–336.

11. I. Bernat, "Pre-morbid personality factors in sustaining and recovering from Combat Stress Reactions," *Psychologia Israel Journal of Psychology* 2, no. 2 (1991): 162–170.

6. Step 4: Get Moving

1. Arthur P. Brief et al., "Inferring the Meaning of Work from the Effects of Unemployment," *Journal of Applied Social Psychology* 25: 8 [April 1995] 693–711; Lin Lean Lim et al., "Economic Performance, Labour Surplus and Enterprise Responses: Results from the China Enterprise Survey," (Labour Market Papers no. 13 ILO Department of Employment and Training, 1996).
2. Brief et al., "Inferring the Meaning of Work. . . ."
3. Brief et al., "Inferring the Meaning of Work. . . ."; J. Iedema and W. Meeus, "The Effects of Work and Relational Mental Incongruity on Identity Formation and Well-Being," *Journal of Adolescence* 21 (1998), 253–264.
4. Brief et al., "Inferring the Meaning of Work. . . ."
5. J. Rost and G. R. Smith, "Return to work after an initial myocardial infarction and subsequent emotional distress," *Archives of Internal Medicine* (1992), 152:381–5.
6. J. Mirowski and C. Ross, "Age and Depression," *Journal of Health and Social Behavior,* 33 (1992), 187–205.
7. E. McAuley, "Physical Activity and Psychosocial Outcomes," *Physical Activity, Fitness, and Health: International Proceedings and Consensus Statement,* ed. C. Bouchard, R. J. Shephard, and T. Stephens (Champaign, IL: Human Kinetics, 1994), 551–568.
8. Lance Armstrong and Sally Jenkins, *Every Second Counts* (New York: Broadway Books, 2004), 3.
9. Lance Armstrong and Sally Jenkins, *It's Not About the Bike: My Journey Back to Life* (New York: Penguin, 2001), 23.
10. Ibid., 86.

7. Step 5: Give Back

1. Shankar Vedantam, "If It Feels Good to Be Good, It Might Be Only Natural," *Washington Post*, May 28, 2007, A1.
2. Claude AnShin Thomas, *At Hell's Gate: A Soldier's Journey from War to Peace* (Boston and London: Shambala Press, 2004), 140.
3. "Cari Lightner September 5, 1966—May 3, 1980," Mothers Against Drunk Driving, May 18, 2007, http://www.madd.org/.
4. Armstrong and Jenkins, *It's Not About the Bike,* 158.

9. Building Resilience to Tragedy

1. Richard G. Tedeschi et al., eds., *Posttraumatic Growth: Positive Changes in the Aftermath of Crisis* (Mahwah, NJ, and London: Lawrence Erlbaum Associates, 1998), 2; P. A. Linley and S. Joseph, "The Human Capacity for Growth Through Adversity" [Comment], *American Psychologist*, 60, no. 3 (2005).
2. Chris Brewin et al., *Hurricane Katrina Community Advisory Group—Baseline Report*, Harvard Medical School Department of Health Care Policy (2006), 17–21, http://www.hurricanekatrina.med.harvard.edu/reports.php.
3. Richard G. Tedeschi and Lawrence G. Calhoun, *Trauma and Transformation: Growing in the Aftermath of Suffering* (Thousand Oaks, CA, London, and New Delhi: Sage), 23–27.
4. Brewin et al., *Hurricane Katrina Community Advisory Group—Baseline Report.*
5. Jane Shakespeare-Finch et al., "The Prevalence of Post-Traumatic Growth in Emergency Ambulance Personnel," *Traumatology* 9, no. 1 (2003), 58–71.

10. Helping Others Get Through Catastrophe

1. Lennis G. Echterling et al., *Crisis Intervention: Promoting Resilience and Resolution in Troubled Times* (Saddle River, NJ: Pearson Education, 2005), 17–25.

2. Ibid., xx.
3. Ibid., 20.
4. Emily Post, *Etiquette in Society, in Business, in Politics and at Home* (New York: Funk & Wagnalls, 1922); available online at http://www.bartleby.com/95/.
5. Joan Rudnicki, "Rules of Grief Etiquette"; available online at http://www.angelfire.com/co3/cbh/COMFORT.html.
6. Friedrich Nietzsche, "The Antichrist," in *The Portable Nietzsche* (New York: Penguin, 1954), 572–573.
7. *The American Heritage Dictionary of the English Language, 4th ed.* (Boston: Houghton Mifflin, 2000).
8. Job 16:4–7.
9. Job 42:7.
10. Job 42:7–17.

11. Survive. Inspire. Thrive!

1. Jules Chametzky, John Felstiner, Hilene Flanzbaum, and Kathryn Hellerstein, *Jewish American Literature: A Norton Anthology* (New York W. W. Norton, 2001); reprinted with permission by My Jewish Learning, http://www.myjewishlearning.com.
2. Elie Wiesel, Nobel Prize Acceptance Speech (Oslo, Norway, December 10, 1986).
3. Helen Keller, *Optimism* (Kila, MT: Kessinger, 2003), 13.
4. Helen Keller, *The Story of My Life* (New York: Bantam, 1990), 18–19.
5. Christopher Reeve, *Still Me,* 267.
6. Nelson Mandela, *Long Walk to Freedom* (New York: Little, Brown and Co., 1994), 391.